PRAYING
WITH
THE CHURCH

PRAYING
WITH
THE CHURCH

ANTHONY M. BUONO

ALBA · HOUSE   NEW · YORK

SOCIETY OF ST. PAUL, 2187 VICTORY BLVD., STATEN ISLAND, NEW YORK 10314

ACKNOWLEDGMENTS

The various prayers from the Liturgy reproduced herein are taken from official liturgical books that are under copyright. They are: Excerpts from the *Sacramentary* © 1985, 1973, International Committee on English in the Liturgy (ICEL); excerpts from the *Rite of Baptism for Children* © 1969, ICEL; excerpts from the *Rite of Confirmation* © 1972, ICEL; excerpts from the *Rite of Penance* © 1973, ICEL; excerpts from the *Rite of Marriage* © 1969, ICEL; excerpts from the *Roman Pontifical* © 1978, ICEL; excerpts from *Pastoral Care of the Sick* © 1982, ICEL; excerpts from the *Liturgy of the Hours* © 1970, 1973, 1975, ICEL; excerpts from the *Book of Blessings* © 1987 ICEL and 1989 United States Catholic Conference. All rights reserved.

Excerpts from Scripture readings of the *Liturgy of the Hours* © 1970 Confraternity of Christian Doctrine. All rights reserved.

Excerpts from the *Enchiridion of Indulgences* © 1969, Catholic Book Publishing Co. All rights reserved.

Library of Congress Cataloging-in-Publication Data

Buono, Anthony M.
    Praying with the church / Anthony M. Buono.
        p.   cm.
    ISBN 0-8189-0579-4
    1. Prayer — Catholic Church.   2. Spiritual life — Catholic authors.
    3. Catholic Church — Liturgy.   I. Title.
    BX2350.2.B85   1990
    264'.02—dc20   90-33607
                                                                   CIP

Designed, printed and bound in the United States of America by the Fathers and Brothers of the Society of St. Paul, 2187 Victory Boulevard, Staten Island, New York 10314, as part of their communications apostolate.

Printing Information:

Current Printing - first digit   1   2   3   4   5   6   7   8   9   10   11   12

Year of Current Printing - first year shown
   1990   1991   1992   1993   1994   1995   1996   1997

CONTENTS

Foreword ix

1. What Is Prayer? 3
   Human Response to the Divine 6
   Encounter with Christ 7
   Application of Christ's Redemption to "My World" 9
   The Four Ends of Prayer 11
   Life in Two Worlds 12

2. The Liturgy — Public Prayer of the Church 15
   The Public Prayer of the Church .16
   Christ in the Liturgy 18
   Content of the Liturgy 19
   The Liturgy Requires Participation 20

3. Liturgical Prayer and Private Prayer 23
   Characteristics of Liturgical Prayer 25
   Praying with the Sentiments of the Liturgy 26
   Praying in Tune with the Liturgical Year 27
   Praying with the Words of the Liturgy 29

4. Praying the Eucharist 33
   Praying the Eucharist 34
   The People's Parts Help Us Pray .36
   Praying in the Liturgy of the Word 37
   Praying in the Liturgy of the Eucharist 39

5. Praying with the Eucharist 43
    Prayerbook of the Church 44
    Makeup of the Missal 46
    Praying with the Words of the Eucharist 51

6. Praying the Sacraments 57
    Christ, the Sacrament of the Encounter with God 59
    Signs of Faith 60
    Personal Encounters with Christ 62
    Praying the Sacraments 64
    Cooperating with Sacramental Grace 66

7. Praying with the Sacraments 69
    Baptism 70
    Confirmation 72
    Penance 73
    Marriage 75
    Holy Orders 77
    Anointing of the Sick 80

8. Praying the Sacramentals 83
    Blessings 85
    Sacramental Actions 87
    Sacramental Words 89
    Sacramental Objects 91
    Sacramental Places 93
    Sacramental Times................................94

9. Praying with the Sacramentals 97
    Praying with Sacramental Blessings 99
    Praying with Indulgenced Prayers 102
    Praying in Sacred Places 106
    Praying in Accord with the Liturgical Seasons 107

10. **Praying the Liturgy of the Hours** 115
A Liturgy "of the Hours" 116
Action and Prayer 118
The Psalms 120
The Readings..................................122
The Responsories...............................123
The Intercessions and Prayers 124

11. **Praying with the Liturgy of the Hours** 127
Praying with the Psalms 129
Praying with the Readings 132
Praying with the Responsories 134
Praying with the Intercessions 136

Afterword 141

FOREWORD

If the unending stream of books, pamphlets, and magazines about prayer is any indication, people today have a deep thirst for prayer. Many seem to follow every prophet who comes up with a new form of praying. They chase after every apostle of prayer with alacrity, abandonment, and hope.

Unfortunately, most seekers after prayer hardly ever advert to the greatest source of prayer in the world — the liturgy. The Church is above all a praying society. Her primary aim is to put people in communication and in union with God: the Father who created us, the Son who redeemed us, and the Holy Spirit who sanctifies us.

Thus, the Second Vatican Council states: "The liturgy is the summit toward which the activity of the Church [and naturally of her members] is directed; at the same time, it is the font from which all her power [and that of her members] flows" (*Constitution on the Sacred Liturgy*, no. 10).

The purpose of this little book is to show how the liturgy can become a wonderful source of prayer for us both in liturgical celebrations and in private praying. The liturgy contains thousands of prayer texts that we can use. Untold treasures lie at our disposal, just waiting to be utilized. They cover every phase of life. The Church has prayers for young and old, rich and poor, sick and healthy, weak and strong, and people of every temperament.

These prayers are saturated with the Word of God and with the Church's centuries-long experience with human nature and human prayer. It would be difficult to surpass them in orthodoxy of doctrine, beauty of language, variety of theme, relevance of content, and understanding of human nature.

It is my belief that every Catholic should know what is in this storehouse of prayer that forms our heritage before looking elsewhere for prayers and should know how to make use of it. This is the initial step in a process that for some will lead to *praying with the Church.*

PRAYING
WITH
THE CHURCH

1

WHAT
IS PRAYER?

Praying is a very common and a very intimate human activity. It is something that countless human beings have done at one time or another since the world began. Christians have prayed billions of times since Jesus taught the apostles how to pray (see Luke 11:1-4).

Prayer is highly personal and at the same time communal, an activity pursued in the privacy of people's minds as well as in the public forum of church and religious assembly. Yet no act of prayer arises from human effort alone. It is our response to God's expression of spontaneous concern.

Praying is one of the most discussed, most promoted, and most analyzed human activities. It is an activity that brings incalculable benefit to those who practice it but also one that is associated with constant distractions, nagging self-doubt, and even a certain amount of despair.

Christian praying is different from all other types. Among its distinctive qualities is the truth that — thanks to the Communion of Saints — *Christians never pray alone*. Whether we know it or not, we always pray *with others*.

In our prayer life, we are consciously or unconsciously

connected with the Church and all her members. We pray with time-honored formulas that originated with the pre-Christians of the Old Testament, the pristine Christians of the New Testament, and the early followers of Christ known as the Fathers.

Every Christian prayer links us — because of our baptismal priesthood — with the liturgy as well as with Mary and the saints in the Body of Christ, which is the Church, and with Christ himself in the Eucharist. At the same time, the human aspect of our prayer unites us with the world, with our Separated Brethren, and with unbelievers of every type.

When we pray, we become one with theologians, poets, and contemplatives who speak, write, and think about God as well as with the suffering in whom Christ calls out to us and the people of our day who look to us for Christ.

All the while our objective is to attain that type of prayer that St. John Chrysostom called the "supreme good" and described so beautifully in the following classic passage:

> Prayer, loving conversation with God, is the supreme good. It is both a relationship with God and union with him. As the eyes of the body are made sharper by the sight of light, so the soul yearning for God is illumined by his ineffable light. Prayer is not the result of an external attitude; it comes from the heart. It is not limited to set hours or minutes, but night and day it is a continuous activity.
>
> It is not enough to direct one's thoughts to God when concentrating exclusively on prayer; even when absorbed in other occupations — such as caring for the poor or some other useful work — it is important to combine the work with desire for and remembrance of God [prayer]. . . .
>
> Prayer is the light of the soul, true knowledge of God and human beings. . . . Through prayer the soul rises

heavenward and embraces the Savior with ineffable love. Like a baby crying out to its mother, it cries out to God, weeping and thirsting for the divine milk. It expresses its deepest desires and receives gifts greater than anything on earth. Prayer, by which we respectfully present ourselves to God, is the joy of the heart and the soul's rest. . . .

Prayer brings the soul to the heavenly fountain, satisfies the soul with this draught, and raises up within it "a spring of water welling up to eternal life" (John 4:14). Prayer gives a real assurance of the good things to come, in faith, and makes present blessings more recognizable. . . .

Do not imagine that prayer consists only in words. It is a leap to God, an inexpressible love that is not of human making, as the Apostle says: "We do not know how to pray as we ought, but the Spirit . . . intercedes with inexpressible groanings" (Romans 8:26).

Such prayer, when the Lord grants it to anyone, is a treasure that cannot be taken away, a heavenly food that satisfies the soul. Those who taste it are filled with an eternal desire for God, such a devouring flame that it enkindles the heart. Let this fire flare up in you in all its fullness, to adorn the dwelling place of the heart with kindness and humility, to make it shine with the light of righteousness, and to polish its floor with good deeds.

Hence, adorn your house, and instead of mosaics decorate it with faith and magnanimity. And as a finishing touch put prayer at the top of your building. Then you will have prepared a house worthy to receive the Lord, as a royal palace, and you yourself will through grace already be possessing him, in a certain manner, in the temple of your soul (*Sixth Homily, On Prayer*: PG 64; 462D-463D. 466).

Human Response to the Divine

One definition of prayer is: "the attitude of heart that under the inspiration of the Holy Spirit opens itself to the Mystery of the Blessed Trinity" (Boniface Baroffio). Prayer is our response to God's self-revelation made to us in Christ and transmitted to us through the Church in the liturgy, the Bible, and daily Christian living.

In prayer we carry out in an eminent manner the priestly function of Jesus Christ, taking over in our hearts the very sentiments of the Mystical Christ — head and members. When we are fully attuned to the Church, our prayer is by its nature an ecclesial prayer.

Prayer is a response to the God who has come — in Jesus Christ — to us. The initiative always comes from God and calls for our obedience of faith, by which we place ourselves completely into God's hands.

It is fair to say that people nowadays pray less than they used to do or at least that they pray with less faith. One of the reasons for this is that they find a divided allegiance within their hearts — to God and to the world. They give themselves to their busy activities for the betterment of the world, yet they feel guilty for their lack of formal prayer.

Such guilt derives from a rather narrow concept of prayer, which sees it as exclusively words, thoughts, and desires addressed to God, a Someone in the Great Beyond, a third entity besides the world and ourselves. This is a God who is purely outside the world rather than within it.

Yet we know that God — Father, Son, and Holy Spirit — is within the world by his immanence. Indeed through Christ, God has become part of this world. Christ penetrates the whole universe, the whole course of history, and humankind in particular. He enlightens every person whether that person knows it or not, and he pervades every part of the cosmos by his dynamic immanence.

Ultimately, prayer is nothing more than an encounter with this Person. Hence, meeting and serving others and also reflecting on and exploring life itself can be called prayer. For in such activities we enounter Christ, though often incognito, in his immanence.

We can say that our every action (no matter how small or how "secular") enables us to be in touch with God. It is God and God alone that devoted Christians pursue through the reality of created things. Our interest lies truly *in* things — but only in absolute dependence upon God's presence in them.

Prayer facilitates seeing God in the world. It enables us to go out of ourselves and rest in him. We refer our lives to another greater than ourselves. It enables us to be what we are, to love ourselves and others in him, and to worship him.

Encounter with Christ

Through prayer we encounter Christ, in whom we are conscious of living with complete joy and freedom, as in the sole real atmosphere of this world. It is the Church which guarantees us a response from God. She does so through her liturgical and sacramental life and her accent on prayer, both personal and liturgical.

To pray is to believe that God is a Person, Someone who listens and who replies and loves us. Prayer is the acceptance of being loved by God. Acceptance entails listening and responding, living a dialogue that should normally increase love.

Prayer thus means to live the Covenant God has made with human beings. It means to enter into the revelation of himself that God the Father has made in the Holy Spirit to the human race through his creation, his chosen people, and ultimately his Son Jesus. In this revelation, God speaks, and human beings speak, and God responds.

The Word became flesh and pitched his tent among us. He is the sacrament of encounter with God, the Great Sign. He is our Bridge to God.

Since he is God, Jesus is the Word of God addressed to humans. Since he is also Man, he is the Response of humans directed to God, the great *Yes* to God, the great *Prayer* to him — throughout his whole life, on Calvary, and in his risen Presence on the altar.

Our great personal and communitarian prayer is the Mass — the Eucharistic Celebration where Christ calls and awaits us so that he can pray in our midst. "He is always able to save those who approach God through him, since he lives forever to make intercession for them. It was fitting that we should have such a high priest: holy, innocent, undefiled, separated from sinners, higher than the heavens" (Hebrews 7:25-26).

Each of the sacraments is thus *both an encounter and a prayer*: an encounter with Christ whose hand touches us through the medium of the Church's rite and an encounter with the Father in a particularly effective prayer — through Jesus Christ, his Son, our Lord— that we may be adopted, reconciled, confirmed, healed, united together in his love, and filled with the Holy Spirit.

The Spirit comes to us in power, light, and love and inspires *prayer and adoration*, the adoration of Christ the Son who cries out to God: "Father." He enables us to pray in Christ, for we are "other Christs." He helps us to utter Christ's prayer: "Father."

Thus, prayer cannot be restricted to sacramental rites or receptions. Just as the sacraments must be lived so that their effects will perdure, so must prayer fill our lives. Prayer is an intervention of God in human space and time; it is also the intervention (so to speak) of human beings in God's space and time.

The sacraments introduce us into *Christian prayer*. This is different from the prayer of pagans or Moslems to the Most High God, all-powerful Creator and Sovereign Master of all things. It is the prayer of Christ — of the Son to his beloved Father in the Spirit.

Christian prayer is also the prayer *to* Christ, our brother, and to Mary his mother, who is also our mother and the mother of the world. Finally, Christian prayer is the prayer to our brothers and sisters in Christ — the saints.

Application of Christ's Redemption to "My World"

It is the power of prayer that keeps us close to Christ and that builds up the Body of Christ. True, the ultimate power comes from the Eucharist, as we shall see in Chapter 4, but all other forms of prayer stem from it — recollection, mental prayer, examination of conscience, purity of intention, vocal prayer, or the sacraments and sacramentals.

These must be utilized to spread the efficacy of the Eucharist in any given situation, time, or place. Just as the Eucharist is the application of Christ's Redemption to the world as a whole, so my prayer flowing from the Eucharist may be looked upon as an application of Christ's Redemption to *my entire world*, transforming it more and more into Christ.

Yet prayer is never carried out in isolation. It is always performed in contact with the real world and in concert with the prayers and aspirations of the whole Mystical Body of Christ. Prayer is not just a set of words, but an attitude that spills over *into action*. It leads us closer to Christ and to fellow human beings.

In the Old Testament, we see the Psalms directing prayer

toward both the temporal and the spiritual salvation of Israel. In the New Testament, we see the stress on the incarnation of love in the heart of the real world. We see this especially in the Lord's Prayer, which associates earth with heaven, the problems of human beings with the coming of God's Kingdom.

Thus, any prayer Christians make is always offered not in their own name or for themselves alone but in the name of and for the whole Body of Christ. Everything we do reflects on that Body either for good or for ill. Our prayer life is no different.

In addition, Christians are not content with merely adoring the beautiful harmonious presence of God in the universe. They inculcate in themselves utter receptivity to cooperate with the God who is operating at each moment in every event. Christian praying starts from our concrete human existence, for only in this can we have any real *relationship* with God.

Persons of prayer are those who habitually say Yes to God in any given situation, while resisting and even transferring the No that the same situation may contain. The response is one that comes from personal freedom, a response given from the Spirit, the inner-dialogue partner, and from the love that he pours forth in our hearts.

For those who pray in this manner, Christ's presence pervades and sustains all things. His power animates all energy. His life seeps into every other life and assimilates it to himself. Every presence makes us feel that Christ is near. Every touch bears the touch of his hand and every necessity transmits an indication of his will. Every affection, every desire, every presence, every light, every depth, every harmony, and every ardor glitters with brilliance in the inexpressible relationship that exists between Christ and us.

The Four Ends of Prayer

Traditionally, prayer is described as possessing a fourfold division, as having four ends or purposes: (1) adoration, (2) praise and thanksgiving, (3) reparation or repentance, and (4) petition or supplication. This division is still useful for it gives the essential elements of the relation of human beings to God.

We *adore* God as the "Ground of our being," our Creator and Lord, on whom we depend for our very existence. We give him *thanks and praise* as our unending Benefactor and our gratuitous Redeemer. We beg him *to forgive* our human failings and strengthen us as our unique Sanctifier. We ask his *help* in our daily existence as our loving Father in accord with the express word of Jesus.

These four ends are all based on *love for God* and in reality never occur alone — they are invariably mingled with one or other of the ends. The division is merely an arbitrary one — to remind us of what we should pray for.

Prayer of petition is often looked down upon as the lowest type of prayer — the "gimme" prayer. As such, it has even fallen into some measure of disuse among certain people. Yet in a very real way all prayer is essentially prayer of petition. Whether we thank God, worship or praise him, or beg his forgiveness, our prayer is always one of "petition" — since we are *asking God for himself*.

Furthermore through prayer of petition we freely contribute to the upbuilding of the universe, and God's concrete manner of caring for the universe will be influenced in some way by our creative choices. We do not ask God to come down and supernaturally transform reality in accord with our wishes. Rather we present our concerns regarding our own creative involvements so that they may enter into his constant reshaping of the universe in response to the free and creative acts of creatures.

God offers possibilities, and human beings actualize them by acting (by prayer). Our prayer is very necessary. It is neither a luxury nor a sham. If we do not pray for such a thing, something will be forever missing even if such an eventuality does come about.

Life in Two Worlds

We live in two worlds at one time — the present reality and an eschatological reality, earth and heaven. Through the Incarnation Christ entered into the present world, and through the Resurrection he entered into the eschatological world. He brought them together so that we may live at once in both — through his grace and the power of the Spirit.

From our vantage point all we see is the disorder of chance events all around us. The future appears chaotic and questionable. But from God's vantage point, everything hangs together, everything makes sense, everything has its own purpose — for these two worlds.

Thus prayer has effects that we do not see — because they affect the totality of events that are influenced by faith. At the same time, God's adaptations of the visible universe to the requirements of our individual soul are done in view of success in heaven and not only a success on earth.

Even if we pray with all our strength, fortune will not necessarily come in the way we wish but in the way that is ordained for us. Petitionary prayer has two levels. The first is when we ask that we may be what we have to be in the circumstances confronting us — as we see things. The second is when we are able to desire what God desires in any situation — as he sees things.

Ultimately, the second level is "letting God be God" in our lives — to a heroic degree. It is a prayer of complete trust in God, an acknowledgment that he knows what is good for us and, if we let him, he will indicate it to us.

The most consoling part for us is that we can pray at all times no matter what we are doing. If we do our actions with a view to building up the Body of Christ, we are always in tune with God, seeing him everywhere and dialoguing with him. We are praying as we live!

2

THE LITURGY — PUBLIC PRAYER
OF THE CHURCH

It is safe to say that during the second half of the 20th century and especially since the Second Vatican Council, Catholics have been living in the "Age of the Liturgy." This does not mean that we are more liturgically conscious, nor even that we have a liturgical spirit and are, so to speak, liturgical persons. It does mean that we now have a greater opportunity to be just that.

The Church, as the Council strongly indicated, is a praying community to whom liturgy is most important, a psalm-singing and praying people, a people of God. The fundamental and characteristic attitude of the Church is, therefore, connected with worship. She is, above all, a religious society. What matters most for her is prayer. Her primary aim is to put people in communication and in communion with God.

Ultimately, the Church's task is to do what Jesus did while on earth. Our Lord was a person of perfect prayer; the Church prays in unison with him. In this collective, public, and official praying, she actualizes in history — through words, love, and sacraments — the Christ of the Gospel, the sole valid and indispensable mediator between God and human beings.

That is why the Church has reformed the liturgy in our day, so that her people may be able to understand it. She urges all her members to participate in the liturgy fully, actively, and consciously — in short, to know, love, and live the liturgy — and to make it part of their everyday lives.

The Public Prayer of the Church

The liturgy — like any general topic — may be defined in a variety of ways. One of the traditional definitions is the following:

> The liturgy is the public worship [prayer] that our Redeemer as Head of the Church renders to the Father as well as the worship that the community of the faithful renders to its Founder, and through him to the Father. It is, in short, the worship rendered by the Mystical Body of Christ in the entirety of its Head and members (Pope Pius XII: *Encyclical on the Sacred Liturgy*, no. 20).

Hence, the liturgy is a form of prayer — indeed, it is the essential prayer between God the Father and his people. The liturgy is a dialogue between God and human beings. God speaks to us in words, signs, and symbols, and we speak to him in the same way. We listen and respond with praise and supplication that terminates in the offering of Christ and our very selves to God (see *Constitution on the Sacred Liturgy*, no. 33).

The liturgy, then, may be legitimately viewed as the primary prayer at our disposal. Through the liturgy we are enabled to grasp the Mystery of Christ and bring it squarely into our lives.

Yet for most of us, liturgy is a rather formidable word — a word that conjures up rites and ceremonies and nonprayerful acts, a word that connotes pomp and pageantry, hardly suited for quiet and earnest prayer with God.

Originally, liturgy denoted a *voluntary work* done for the people. The Greek translation of the Jewish Scriptures completed in the 3rd century B.C. and known as the *Septuagint* turned this word into a reference to the *priestly worship* carried on in the Temple.

The early Church and the Fathers used it for a service of worship in which each member of the community offers to God on behalf of all in accord with his or her role. By the Middle Ages, it came to denote the official worship of the Church.

Thus, liturgy is a divine work entrusted to the people of God. It is the carrying on of the *work of Christ* by his Church in union with him. Those who were not privileged to encounter Christ in his earthly life can now encounter him in his glorified state through the liturgy and can unite with him in his sacrifice to the Father made once and for all.

Viewed in this way, the liturgy loses most of its formidable character. It comes across to us as it truly is: a key to life, a call to union, a blessing brimming with gifts, a petition filled with hope, the extension of the Paschal Mystery to all ages and all peoples, and indeed to the whole universe.

It is our privilege as Christians to be able to take part in this prayer of the Church — through our baptism that made us *universal priests*. It is our privilege to take part in this prayer — through a *hierarchical order* that is essential to it. It is our privilege to take part in this prayer — in a *communal fashion* as members of the Church community. It is our privilege to be *sanctified* by this prayer — through insertion into Christ's Paschal Mystery. Finally, it is our privilege to be instructed by this prayer — as part of those to whom God speaks *through Christ in the Spirit.*

Christ in the Liturgy

God created all things and all people in view of Christ. Everything that went before him looked toward Christ, and everything that has come after him looks back to Christ.

The endless ages that went before the birth of Christ are not devoid of him. They are pervaded by his influence. It was the ferment of his conception that set the cosmic masses moving and controlled the first currents of life in the world. It was the preparation for his birth that accelerated human progress and human development on earth.

Christ's coming called for all the fearsome, anonymous toil of primitive humanity, for the long drawn-out beauty of Egypt, for Israel's anxious expectation, for the slowly distilled fragrance of Eastern mysticism, and for the endlessly refined wisdom of the Greeks and the Romans.

We have much in common with the peoples of the nations that looked toward Christ in ancient times. But we are also more fortunate. Our faith is based on many more tangibles. It is enlightened, strong, and well-founded. When coupled with the liturgy of the Church it enables us to attain the expectation of our hearts.

Jesus the God-Man is the High Priest of the human race who achieved true worship — perfect dialogue — with his heavenly Father. He did so by offering his life in the flesh (his "Physical Body," so to speak), and by dying and rising again. This is the Paschal Mystery.

Jesus did not relegate his actions just to the people of his time. He prolonged them for all succeeding ages through his Mystical Body, the Church. In this way, people of all times come in contact with him, render fitting worship to the Father through the Holy Spirit, and obtain the saving benefits Jesus achieved once and for all.

The Church celebrates this liturgy, this praise of God,

day and night on behalf of all. She prays for the salvation of the world and fosters thanksgiving and praise to God. Every Sunday she keeps the memory of our Lord's Paschal Mystery, and she continues to sanctify time and consecrate it to God by the Liturgical Year. She unfolds the whole Mystery of Christ — from the Incarnation and Birth to the Crucifixion, the Resurrection, the Ascension, the day of Pentecost, and even to the expectation of the Lord's Second Coming.

Through the liturgy, we enter into the events of Christ's life. We encounter Christ — not in the flesh but in his Mysteries. And these have the power to sanctify us now as much as they had the power to sanctify those who met Jesus in the flesh on earth.

Content of the Liturgy

The liturgy may be viewed as a dialogue, an exchange of words between God and his people. But it is even more. It is an action in which God acts and his people become involved. In this communication, the liturgy makes use of signs as well as words. It requires bodily attitudes, comprises gestures and actions, makes use of things, is carried out in places, confects objects and consecrates them.

Some of these signs are so-called natural signs. They reproduce the language that God, as it were, has inserted in creation and the human heart. But most of them are Biblical signs. They are the signs that Jesus himself used for the Mass and the sacraments as well as those that the rest of the Scriptures show being used by our predecessors in the faith.

Indeed, the liturgy has been called the *Bible in action*, for the Bible permeates every part of the liturgical rites. The liturgy includes Bible passages (readings), Bible chants (antiphons and hymns), Bible formulas (greetings, acclamations, and institution narrative), Bible allusions (prayers), and Bible instruction (homily) as well as extemporaneous prayers of the individual community that are Bible-inspired.

The principal celebrant of the liturgy is Christ himself. The second celebrant is the general body of the faithful and the local community assembled in the liturgy. The third celebrant is the bearer of the official priesthood who stands at the altar.

In the liturgy each person has an office to perform as a result of the universal priesthood received at baptism. The people take their part by means of acclamations, responses, psalmody, antiphons, songs, as well as by actions, gestures, bodily attitudes, and a reverent silence at the proper time.

The liturgy contains instruction in the faith, for the Church teaches as she sanctifies. In the liturgy God speaks to his people and Christ is still proclaiming his Gospel.

The liturgy comprises the sacred rites of the Eucharist (both Mass and sacrament), baptism, confirmation, penance, holy orders, marriage, and anointing of the sick as well as the Liturgy of the Hours and the sacramentals.

The liturgy is directly related to our daily life. It is intended to keep alive in the whole Christian community the meaning of our lives as Christians. In the liturgy we find the power and the strength to make Christ present and active in our world. In our daily lives we bear witness to Christ's enduring love for all people and his unflagging concern for the betterment of humankind here on earth. By our faith in the Second Coming of Christ, which the liturgy holds up constantly before our eyes, we keep alive in the world the blessed hope that human existence has ultimate and eternal significance.

The Liturgy Requires Participation

Participation in the liturgy is both the right and the duty of the faithful by reason of their baptism and confirmation and/or

holy orders, which give each a share in the priesthood of
Christ. The laity have a universal priesthood and the priests
have a ministerial one. The Second Vatican Council stressed
this point:

> Mother Church earnestly desires that all the faithful
> should be led to that full, conscious, and active participa-
> tion in liturgical celebrations that is demanded by the
> liturgy. Such participation by the Christian people as a
> "chosen race, a royal priesthood, a holy nation, a re-
> deemed people" (1 Peter 2:9; see 2:4f), is their right and
> duty by reason of their baptism (*Constitution on the
> Sacred Liturgy*, no. 14).

Participation in anything entails rapport, relationship,
communication, and union among other things. In the liturgy
this means everyone must do what pertains to him or her by
reason of the order to which he or she belongs or the role
assigned to each. It also means that each person should have
the right dispositions of faith and love and cooperation with
divine grace and effects.

Participation in the liturgy thus becomes a personal response in the unique mystical presence of the Church to the
call of the Father in, with, and through Christ by the power of
the Holy Spirit.

The Church insists that this participation must have three
qualities.

It must be *full*. The people must be perfectly attuned to
the objective of the celebration. They must also involve all the
faculties at their command: mind, heart, and soul as well as
body with tongue and lips, hands and feet, arms and legs, eyes
and ears.

It must be *conscious*. The people must be fully aware of
what they are doing, actively engaged in the service, and
enriched by its effects. They must be eager to know and
understand all the ramifications of the service.

Finally, this participation must be *active*. The people must not be present with devout attendance or simple assistance. They are not to be simple spectators, no matter how interested. They must be totally involved in the service by their actions — responding, praying, and worshiping.

It is obvious that this type of participation is an ideal that the people scarcely ever attain. Nonetheless, it should be pursued. Even when they fail, they will reap fruits from it. The closer they get to the ideal, the closer they will come to God and to one another and the greater will be the fruits they receive for their lives.

3

LITURGICAL PRAYER
AND PRIVATE PRAYER

A story is told about two priests who went fishing. While waiting for the fish, they began to say their office, called the *Liturgy of the Hours*. Out of the blue, a storm appeared and threatened to drown them. The older priest seized the oars in a panic and shouted to the other: "Put that book down and start praying."

The punch line of this apocryphal tale does not sink in until we reflect on the fact that the *Liturgy of the Hours* is the liturgical prayer of the Church. The priest was thus praying already — in the name of the Church. However, he felt the need to pray in his own words — he felt the need for private prayer in this crisis.

Liturgical prayer does not meet every human need, nor is it intended to do so. One of the graphic indications of this fact is found in the Catholics who didn't like the new Mass when it was first introduced — because they couldn't pray during the service anymore.

They had been accustomed to reciting private prayers during the Latin Mass. Now, with the return to the language of the people and the demands of active participation, they found it too distracting to perform personal devotions during the celebration of the Eucharist.

In a sense all Catholics were in this position regarding the Mass. Their whole outlook had to change. They had to find the opportunity for personal prayer apart from the liturgy. For liturgical prayer and private prayer are both necessary, and one cannot supply for the other.

Liturgical prayer is meant to be generous, outgoing, and largely "other-centered." As such, it cannot satisfy personal needs that are legitimate. Private prayer, on the other hand, is self-directed and self-oriented. It does not intend to replace communal liturgical prayer.

God our Father welcomes us into his home, the Church, as his family, but he also invites us to communicate with him individually in private. Private prayer is inappropriate during the communal celebration of the Eucharist. It is, however, much needed to prepare for liturgical prayer and to prolong its effects in our lives.

Careful attention to this important fact will enable us to grow in our prayer life in line with the teaching of the Church. We will participate completely at liturgical celebrations and pray more fervently in private.

The Second Vatican Council stressed the importance of both types of prayer: "The spiritual life is not confined to participation in the liturgy [that is, to liturgical prayer]. Christians are assuredly called to pray with their brothers and sisters, but they must also enter into their rooms to pray to the Father in secret (see Matthew 6:6); indeed, according to the teaching of the apostle Paul, they should pray without ceasing" (*Constitution on the Sacred Liturgy*, no. 12).

The Church's sole stipulation is that our private prayer must be liturgy-minded. According to the document cited above, "prayers and devotions of the Christian people are to be so drawn up that they harmonize with the liturgical seasons,

accord with the sacred liturgy, are in some measure derived
from it, and lead the people back to it. "

Characteristics of Liturgical Prayer

The liturgy always prays to the Father through the Son in
the Holy Spirit. This is the pattern of all liturgical prayer. And
it should be the pattern for all our prayers. It is the so-called
trinitarian-christological dimension of Christian prayer:

> Every good gift comes to us from the Father, through the
> medium of Jesus Christ his incarnate Son, in the pres-
> ence of the Holy Spirit; and likewise, it is in the presence
> of the Holy Spirit, through the medium of Jesus Christ the
> incarnate Son, that everything must return to the Father
> and be reunited with its end, the Most Blessed Trinity
> (Cyprian Vagaggini, *Theological Dimensions of the Litur-
> gy*, p. 191).

Accordingly, no matter what prayer we use, it should
always be undergirded by the liturgical approach — God as
Father, Jesus as Mediator, and Holy Spirit as Sanctifier.

This type of prayer is not only the most Christian but also
the most beneficial for us. It makes us the object of the action
and gives us edification. It is concerned with great religious
themes and is highly formalized. It follows an elaborate rhythm
of instruction, logic, and prayer. It is elevated, living, and
changing.

Perhaps most important of all, liturgical prayer aids our
self-fulfillment and our Christian fulfillment. The liturgy
achieves a balance between the individual and the community.
It obtains for the person the community outlook that is necessary for the prompting of grace.

In Christianity, the subject of grace is the person in a love of God that, like every love, is incommunicably personal and in a faith that is the supreme act of an inviolable freedom. As a member of the Mystical Body whose Head is Christ, the person retains total autonomy.

Yet this religious exaltation of the person on the part of the liturgy is realized only in the regimen, rhythm, and fusion of community. This community is not only the spiritual community of the Body of Christ but also the fraternal community that expresses the Body visibly.

Community expresses the necessary vehicle for the Christian life, for the development of the person, both in grace and in nature. Liturgical truth thus coincides with human truth.

Praying with the Sentiments of the Liturgy

The object of all liturgy is a *liturgical life* or, as some call it, *vital prayer*, the prayer of life. Our liturgical prayer is real only if our everyday lives are touched and molded by it into truly Christian lives. The liturgy, with all its beauty and solemnity, would be valueless for us if our lives were not part of it. In the same way, our lives would be totally secular if they did not have the liturgy to form and fashion them.

A principal way of bringing about this vital praying is by participating so fully, actively, and consciously in liturgical celebrations, especially the Sunday Eucharist, that the liturgy will automatically overflow into our lives. And a way of doing so is to go over the liturgical texts beforehand so that we can better participate in the service itself.

We can also take the liturgical texts as the source for our prayer-meditation. In this way the Paschal Mystery that permeates the liturgy will be ever before us. In doing so, however, we must remember to emphasize four features in our prayer that were set forth by Pope Paul VI.

Our prayer should have a Biblical basis. It should take its start from the Bible, dwell on Bible themes, and end with authentic Bible teaching. It should lead us to listen to the Word of God and respond to it with Biblically inspired words and ideas.

Our prayer should also possess a liturgical imprint. It should take its inspiration from the liturgical seasons and feasts. In this way, we will be better prepared to take part in future liturgies.

Our prayer should manifest an ecumenical spirit. It should avoid every type of exaggeration and incorrect practice that would hinder Christian unity. It should lead us unerringly to Christ the Head of all Christians and make us better disposed toward our "Separated Brethren."

Our prayer should reflect the human situation. It should lead us to the holiness possible to our state of life, based on our response to the Word of God. It should also keep us current about the new and valuable perspectives uncovered by the human sciences in our day.

By praying in this manner, we will combine the prayer of the heart and the prayer of worship. Our private prayer will never be cut off from our liturgical prayer. We will take full advantage of the Church's way of praying and the Church's way of understanding and appreciating the central mysteries of our faith.

Praying in Tune with the Liturgical Year

Another way of bringing about this vital prayer is by being in tune with the Liturgical Year to such an extent that its rhythm-themes will dictate our sentiments of prayer throughout the year.

In ordinary human life, a living memory can be a major

force for good or evil. The remembrance of a beloved parent
can impel us to write a letter, set up an award, or offer a prayer
for eternal rest. The memory of an acclaimed stage performance can strengthen an aging actor and move him to overcome
pressing problems.

The liturgy is the living memory of the Church, the
community of witnesses to Christ. Through the liturgy, the
Church recalls the Mysteries of Christ. In doing so, she is
sustained by Christ the Son of God and enabled to span time.
She feels the power of his mysteries in her members who are
thereby sanctified and moved to act.

Over the course of centuries, the Church has structured
this Memory into a yearly cycle commemorating one or other
event of her Savior's life. In traversing this Liturgical Year, we
are able to be more closely conformed to Christ by prayer as
well as other means — pious practices, instruction, and works
of penance and mercy.

Hence, during Advent, our prayer should look forward
with anticipation to a new coming of Christ in our lives, just as
the people of old awaited the purifying coming of the Messiah.
This is his *coming in mystery* to counterbalance his *coming in
history* in the past and his *coming in glory* in the future.

During the Christmas Season, we should rejoice over
Christ's triple coming with all the benefits it entails for us. We
thank him for obtaining salvation for us by his first coming; we
ask him to apply that salvation to us by this his second coming;
and we pray that he will complete that salvation for us at his
third coming upon our death.

During the Lenten Season, we should do penance and
prepare to "die to self" with Christ. Our prayer should be to
apply ourselves to eradicating all that is bad in us so that we
may be "new persons" for Christ on Easter.

During the Easter Season, we should be filled with joy
over Christ's saving act and his glorification through his Resur-

rection. Our prayer should celebrate the magnificent victory over sin and death that God has made possible for us in Christ.

During Ordinary Time, we should strive to encounter Jesus in his ceaseless efforts to proclaim the Good News. Our prayer should be to strive to perfect his works in our day through the power of the Holy Spirit.

In this annual cycle, the Church also proclaims the Paschal Mystery achieved in the saints who have suffered and been glorified with Christ. Our prayer should help us take the saints as exemplars of some aspect of Christ's holiness and as intercessors for us before God's throne.

Through a modicum of effort we can take hold of the Liturgical Year in our prayer life and live it to the full. In this way we may derive its threefold fruit — to know Jesus, to imitate Jesus, and to live in, with, and through Jesus.

Praying with the Words of the Liturgy

A third way of bringing about this vital prayer is by praying with the very words of the liturgy. The liturgy contains thousands of prayer texts that we can use, ranging from the most known ("God, come to my assistance; Lord, make haste to help me" — from the *Liturgy of the Hours*) to the least known (the doxological conclusion to the Our Father at Mass: "Deliver us Lord, from every evil, / and grant us peace in our day. / In your mercy keep us free from sin / and protect us from all anxiety / as we wait in joyful hope / for the coming of our Savior, Jesus Christ. / For the kingdom, the power, and the glory are yours, now and for ever").

The Church's treasury of liturgical prayer is great indeed. Among other things it contains all the greatest prayers from the Bible, starting with the Psalms. Think of Psalm 23, The Good Shepherd, or Psalm 130, Out of the Depths. They are classics not only of Catholic literature but of world literature!

In the Psalter God puts on our lips the words he wants to hear and indicates to us the dimensions of prayer:

> The Psalms recall to mind the truths revealed by God to the chosen people, which were at one time frightening and at another filled with wonderful tenderness; they keep repeating and fostering the hope of the promised Redeemer, which in ancient times was kept alive with song, either around the hearth or in the stately Temple; they show forth in splendid light the prophesied glory of Jesus Christ: first, his supreme and eternal power, then his lowly coming to this earthly exile, his kingly dignity and priestly power, and finally his beneficent labors and the shedding of his blood for our redemption.
>
> In a similar way they express the joy, the bitterness, the hope and fear of our hearts and our desire of loving God and hoping in him alone as well as our mystic ascent to divine tabernacles (Pope Pius XII: *Encyclical on the Sacred Liturgy*, no. 148).

The liturgy also contains the prayers of Jesus, starting with the magnificent Our Father. These can be an inspiration to all of us as we carry on the work of Christ through the task given each of us.

Other prayers contained in this liturgical treasury are those of the early Church. Some of these are the prayers found in the letters of St. Paul and St. Peter as well as the wonderful *Magnificat*, the prayer of Our Lady. By making use of such prayers we can renew in ourselves the fervent faith and single-minded outlook that were characteristic of the early Christians.

The liturgy also contains the best prayers of Christians of all ages — up to the present time. It has prayers of St. Leo the Great (5th century) and St. Gregory the Great (7th century), which exude true doctrine and authentic holiness. It brings before us the classic prayers of the Middle Ages known as Sequences — like the *Stabat Mater* ("The Mother Was Standing"), which is recited during the Stations of the Cross.

The great Eucharistic prayers of St. Thomas Aquinas also find a place in the liturgy. These include the *Lauda, Sion, Salvatorem* ("Zion, Praise Your Savior") in the Mass for the Body and Blood of Christ and the splendid Prayers before and after Communion.

Finally, the Church has added modern prayers that are equally useful. The *Liturgy of the Hours* contains new Intercessory prayers that can be utilized with maximum effect in applying liturgy to our lives in the world.

The list above gives us only a glimpse at the wonderful treasury of prayers that the Church has amassed for us over the centuries. Suffice it to say that we will never be at a loss for prayers if we have recourse to the time-tested formulas that the liturgy offers us.

4

PRAYING
THE EUCHARIST

If we were to ask Catholics what the greatest prayer was, it is highly likely that we would receive a host of different answers ranging from the *Our Father* to the *Twenty-Third Psalm* to the *Prayer of St. Francis*, among others. But it is very unlikely that many of them would reply: the Eucharist. That is because we hardly ever think of the Eucharist as a prayer.

Yet that is precisely what the Eucharist is — a prayer, and indeed the greatest of all prayers. The Eucharist achieves the four ends that make up any prayer — and it does so in the greatest possible way. For it is prayed in union with the Son of God made Man, Jesus Christ, who gave himself so that all might be able to pray with him.

The Eucharist is first of all a prayer of *praise and adoration*. We *adore* God as our Creator and Lord, and we *praise* him for the countless benefits he has heaped on all human beings — beginning with life, intelligence, freedom, and the opportunity to be his heirs.

The Eucharist is a prayer of *thanksgiving*. We thank God for his constant care of us, for his goodness in creating and sanctifying us, and for all his interventions in the life of his people. We also show our gratitude for all that he has done for us as individuals.

The Eucharist is a prayer of *petition*. We ask God to bestow his blessings on all human beings, on his Church, and on us as individuals. It is Jesus who asks for us and the Holy Spirit in whom we ask. How can our prayer fail to be heard by God the Father?

Finally, the Eucharist is a prayer of *repentance and atonement*. We offer it to make satisfaction for all sins committed against God as well as our own sins. We are thus enabled to achieve holiness for all and for ourselves.

Most important of all, the Eucharist is not an individual prayer. It is a prayer of the whole Church — a community prayer. In this heart of Christian prayer, we encounter Christ — the revealer of the Father in the Spirit.

Indeed, we receive the Whole Christ: his Word, his Body, his Spirit. His Word tells us how we are to speak to God. His Body and Blood is the sole offering that is pleasing to the Father. And his Spirit is the one who teaches us how to pray and what to pray for.

If we but join in the Eucharist wholeheartedly, our prayer life will be on its way to being complete. It will naturally have to be completed by private prayer. But we will have taken a giant step toward a prayer-filled life by "praying" the Eucharist.

Praying the Eucharist

If the Eucharist is our greatest prayer, then we should *actively pray* it. The only way to do this is to participate at it fully, actively, and consciously. The Church insists on this point:

> The Church . . . earnestly desires that Christ's faithful,
> when present at this Mystery of Faith, should not be there
> as silent spectators; on the contrary, through a good
> understanding of the rites and prayers they should take
> part in the sacred action *conscious* of what they are doing,
> with *devotion* and *full collaboration (Constitution on the
> Sacred Liturgy*, no. 47).

The Eucharist is a prayer-action of the community assembled together to render worship to God. As we have seen,
this requires both external and internal participation on the
part of all present. For it is the whole person who praises God
and who prays.

Of course, we should never be preoccupied solely with
external responses to every word or action of the celebrant and
ministers. What we should do is make an *effort* to respond
whenever we can, without making our response a mere formal-
ity with no inner attitude behind it. By dwelling on our parts
(the *people's parts*) at Mass, we can participate fully, actively,
and consciously as desired by the Church.

A diligent performance of our parts at the Eucharist
fortified by a true spiritual outlook will ensure that every
Eucharist will also be a *prayer* for us. It will not be merely an
empty ceremony or external display. It will create a praying
relationship between us and God and between us and other
human beings.

This type of full participation will help us to pray with
Christ and with the Church — to place their concerns before
the Father, to pray as part of a community and as part of the
universal Church.

It will also enable us to insert our own individual concerns into the petitions of the Church — as she specifically
wants us to do. For example, we can add our petitions to those
of the Church in the Opening Prayer, in the Prayer of the

Faithful, and in the intercessions of the Eucharistic Prayer.
We thereby individualize those prayers and universalize our
petitions! Our prayer will be linked with the prayers of Christ
and his Church, and their prayers will be linked with ours.

Finally, the Eucharist also offers select times during
which we as individuals can commune with God and Christ
silently but in common (at the Silence after Communion, for
example). All we need do is take good advantage of them and
our own private prayer cannot help but be enriched.

The People's Parts Help Us Pray

The Church has done a masterful job in inserting mean-
ingful and inspiring parts for the people all through the new rite
of celebrating the Eucharist. A conscientious attempt to carry
out those parts with understanding and fervor will inevitably
help us pray the Eucharist.

The "new" Mass (like the "old") is composed of an
Ordinary and a *Proper*. The Ordinary can be termed the outline
or framework of the Mass structure. It indicates the texts and
ceremonies that occur and the correct sequence they should
follow. It contains the texts that form part of almost every
celebration.

The Proper contains the texts that vary according to the
liturgical seasons (Advent, Christmas, Lent, Easter, and Ordinary Time) or according to the particular feast (of a saint who
was a martyr, or a virgin, or a Doctor of the Church, and so
forth).

In both the Ordinary and the Proper there are texts and
actions assigned to the different participants in the Eucharist
— the celebrant, the various ministers, and the people. This
accounts for the use of the term *people's parts*.

The Mass is divided into two logical components, the

Liturgy of the Word and the Liturgy of the Eucharist. In the Liturgy of the Word, we exercise our role by encountering Christ in the proclamation of God's Word and by preparing for and responding to that Word. In the Liturgy of the Eucharist, we exercise our role by actively participating in the renewal of the sacrifice of the cross through our acclamations and responses as well as by our intimate union with the glorified Lord in Communion.

The Mass is further divided into five minor components — two in the Liturgy of the Word and three in the Liturgy of the Eucharist. These are: (1) the Introductory Rites; (2) the Word of God; (3) the Preparation of the Gifts; (4) the Eucharistic Prayer; and (5) the Eucharistic Banquet. Each has its own particular function and specific message for us.

The Ordinary people's parts occur throughout every division of the Mass, and the Proper people's parts occur in all except the Eucharistic Prayer, which is the priestly prayer beyond compare. These parts are so structured as to elicit definite sentiments from us and insure our full participation.

Praying in the Liturgy of the Word

The Introductory Rites — Keynote. The Entrance Hymn (and Entrance Antiphon, which is substituted when there is no singing) is usually regarded as setting the tone for the particular celebration of the day. We acclaim Jesus (in the person of the priest) who comes to reenact and re-present his saving sacrifice for us and to invite us to partake of his sacrificial meal — to become one in him.

In the Ordinary parts that follow, we exchange greetings with the priest and ask God to purify us before we hear his Word and celebrate his Eucharist. At the same time, through this Penitential Rite we ask forgiveness of one another so that we may offer this Eucharist with complete solidarity.

Now we offer praise and thanksgiving by means of beautiful and ancient Ordinary texts directed to Christ: the Kyrie, a litany-like plea to Jesus (which can also be used in the Penitential Rite) and the Gloria. The latter is directed to the Father and concludes with praise to the Trinity. However, its body is a lyrical praise of the incarnate Son, our Redeemer and our Intercessor with the Father.

The Introductory Rites conclude with the celebrant reciting the Opening Prayer in our name. By our response ("Amen") we give our ringing assent to everything that has gone before. This Prayer gathers together the sentiments expressed in the Entrance Hymn (and Entrance Antiphon) and recasts them in a formal petition to the Father in the name of the People of God relying on the merits of Christ his Son.

The Word of God — Response. Christ now comes among us in the proclamation of the Word of God. We have an Ordinary response after each of the three readings ("Thanks be to God" after the first two and "Praise to you, Lord Jesus Christ" after the third), two Ordinary dialogue-responses at the beginning of the Gospel ("And also with you"; "Glory to you, Lord Jesus Christ"), and two Proper chants. The latter used to be termed Intervenient Chants and are now known as the Responsorial Psalm and the Alleluia or Gospel Acclamation.

We use the Responsorial Psalm to respond to the First Reading, which is usually taken from the Prophets of the Old Testament or the Letters of the Apostles of the New Testament. The Responsorial Psalm presents us with a sure way of making a positive response to the Word we have just heard.

By the Alleluia we look forward to the Gospel message. We acclaim the Christ who comes in our midst during the proclamation of his Word. It forms the people's culmination of the Liturgy of the Word — short, yet packed with meaning.

We now go to meet Christ as he becomes present once

again in the proclamation of his Gospel. Our response after the Gospel bears out this point: "Praise to you, Lord Jesus Christ." It is to Christ that we are speaking. It is Christ that we have encountered.

After listening reverently to God's Word, we listen to the updating of that Word (to our circumstances of life) by the Homily that is preached. We then voice our acceptance of this Word in the Nicene Creed. This is a long and beautiful profession of faith that is one of the people's parts of the Ordinary and dates back to the 4th century.

Here too prayers are interspersed relating this part of the Mass to actual circumstances: these make up the Prayer of the Faithful. When correctly composed, the list of petitions takes its starting point from the Bible texts just proclaimed and the response just elicited. In that way we can readily give our assent to the sentiments voiced. We do so by the Amen uttered at the end of the concluding prayer said by the celebrant. By this same Amen, we also assent to all that has been done during this division of the Mass.

Praying in the Liturgy of the Eucharist

The Preparation of the Gifts — Offering. The second major division of Mass begins with a processional chant that introduces and sets the tone for the Preparation of the Gifts. It is sung while a few members of the asembly are bringing the gifts to the altar from which the sacrifice of the Mass will be effected — the bread and wine as well as the sacred vessels. They are our gifts to God that will be turned into his Gift (Jesus) to us.

These gifts not only encompass the sacred vessels and utensils that are brought up; they also embody all the monetary gifts that we offer for the good of the community (for liturgy, counseling, education, and the like). Perhaps most important of all, they also embrace all the joys and sorrows that the present day or present week will bring for us and the community as a whole.

We symbolically place them in the hands of the members of the Offertory Procession to bring them to the altar to be offered in our name in this holy sacrifice. Then certain that our offering is accepted, we will be able to go on in our pilgrim journey fortified by the graces stemming from this Eucharist.

Just before the end of this part, the celebrant exhorts us to join wholeheartedly in his sacrifice and ours. We immediately give our affirmative response. We thus vocalize what we have already symbolized by our gifts in the Offertory Procession.

Finally, the celebrant adds the "summing up" Prayer over the Gifts in the name of the whole assembly. It is usually related to the Offertory Hymn. As we voice our Amen, we assent to the Prayer and to all that has been done in this part of Mass.

The Eucharistic Prayer — Encounter. The Eucharistic Prayer opens with the Introductory Dialogue that helps us get into the spirit of this "heart of the Mass." We are invited to praise and thank God; we give our prompt response that it is not only good but right to do so.

The Preface follows and lists the particular reason for praising God on this day — in addition to the overriding reasons found in Salvation History. We join our sentiments to those given in the Preface by voicing another praise of God with the magnificent Holy, Holy, Holy. We stress that the earth as well as heaven is filled with God's glory — and that glory will increase as we continue this Eucharist.

We go on to join the celebrant silently as he calls upon the Holy Spirit to make holy our sacrifice, and we enter the narrative of the Last Supper. By it, we — so to speak — are given a front seat at the Lord's Institution of the Eucharist. The celebrant in Christ's person repeats the words and actions of Christ, allowing us to encounter Jesus at the high point of his sacrificial giving on earth.

Christ becomes present in a new and wonderful way, and we address him in the beautiful words of the Memorial Acclamation. We should do everything we can to pronounce them with outward reverence and inner conviction. The four formularies that may be used constitute what the Mass is all about. Christ has redeemed us *in history*. He is with us now *in mystery*. He will come to us again *in glory*. Every Mass is our little Easter.

The Eucharistic Prayer recalls the saving events of Christ and then lists the "us" for whom the sacrifice is being offered; the servants of God, our relatives, friends, and benefactors who are Christians as well as all people, living and dead.

Then the concluding Doxology gives glory to the Father, through the Son, in the Holy Spirit. We rise and voice our full endorsement of this sentiment through our Great Amen. We assent to all that has gone before. We have encountered Christ. We now want to offer ourselves with, through, and in him, and we eagerly look forward to our union with him in Communion.

The Eucharistic Banquet — Union. This part of Mass is also governed by the people's processional chant — which this time does not introduce it. We prepare for Communion by reciting our Ordinary parts: the Our Father, the responses to the Prayer for Peace, the Sign of Peace, and the Lamb of God (a prayer for pardon and peace), while the celebrant makes a quiet preparation for Communion. Then with the celebrant we acknowledge our unworthiness to receive such a Visitor in the words of the Centurion of the Gospel: "Lord, I am not worthy. . . ."

At this point the Communion Antiphon (or Communion

Hymn) is recited or sung. This text gives us the particular
nuance for the reception of Communion each day. It allows us
to vary our reflections for receiving Christ from day to day in
accord with the Liturgical Year.

After Communion the celebrant performs the ablutions
and a period of silence follows — for personal or public
thanksgiving. Then the celebrant says the Prayer after Communion in the name of all. It sums up the sentiments of those
present, inspired by the Communion Antiphon. We concur in
these sentiments by our response Amen, which also gives our
assent to all that has been done in this part of Mass.

Finally, the celebrant blesses the assembly in the name of
the Triune God and sends us forth to bring Christ into our daily
lives and relationships. We answer with a last word of assent:
"Thanks be to God," and then sing a Recessional Hymn,
officially closing the celebration in a customary way.

Even a cursory look at the explanation given above will
show how many helps are built into the Eucharist itself to help
us participate at Mass — to pray it, so to speak. All we need is
to simply pay attention and be of goodwill. The rite of the
Church will do the rest.

5

PRAYING
WITH THE EUCHARIST

B esides *praying the Eucharist*, we are able to pray *with* the Eucharist, as we have mentioned. This means making the Eucharistic texts our prayer. The best way to do so is by the use of a Missal.

At social gatherings when a lull appears in the proceedings, the old bromide inevitably pops up: "If you were marooned on a desert island, what single book would you want?" And the answers are as varied as there are people. Some opt for the Bible, others for Shakespeare, still others for a "how-to-survive" book, and so on.

Never does one hear the word "Missal." Indeed, most Catholics hardly know what the name means anymore. Why in the world would anyone want that book? The reason, of course, is that the Missal provides food for our spiritual life. It enables us to live spiritually even while we strive to find sustenance to live materially.

The Missal is a service book for the Eucharistic celebration. It contains the rites and prayers by which the Paschal Mystery of Christ's death and resurrection is made present in the religious worship of the people of God in assembly.

The Missal also contains the rites and prayers for the sacraments. It thus places them in the proper perspective for those who make use of the Missal. It shows the true relationship of all the sacraments to the Eucharist and to each other.

Obviously, the Missal imparts a liturgical culture that no other book can do. It provides the texts and rubrics or directions that bring out the essence of worship in an existential way. These express what human language and signs offer to God in praise and thanksgiving and they proclaim God's saving acts in the past, present, and future.

The Missal also has other qualities. It gives us a *knowledge of the Mystery of Faith*. As such, it can be called a textbook of Church teachings. But it is not a dead textbook. It is a living instrument of Christian knowledge — because it is used in the living liturgy.

The Missal is a *prayerbook* as well. It teaches us to pray with the "mind of the Church," which is none other than the mind of Jesus: "Whoever listens to you listens to me" (Luke 10:16). We can be sure that any prayer found in the Missal is a prayer that is pleasing to God.

Finally, the Missal is an excellent *introduction to the Bible*. It provides us with the Church's commentary on the Word of God and shows us the Bible in action in the liturgy.

It is the Missal, then, that is the *must* book for every Catholic. It is our *Catechism*, our *Prayerbook*, our *Bible*, and our *Book of Worship* all rolled into one! The Missal is our sure guide to a Eucharistic spirituality, which is the basis for an authentic Christian life.

Prayerbook of the Church

The liturgy is a veritable school of prayer. This means the Missal is the Church's basic prayerbook, an initiation into

Christian prayer. A diligent use of this treasury of prayer can make us people of prayer.

The Missal tells us *why we should pray*. God is our Lord and Father who wants us to stay in touch with him through prayer: "[Jesus] told them a parable about the necessity for them to pray always without becoming weary" (Luke 18:1). With prayer we can obtain our salvation and even temporal benefits: "Ask and you will receive; seek and you will find; knock and the door will be opened to you" (Luke 11:9).

The Missal instills in us *what we should pray for*. It sets before us the twin aims of every liturgical service: the glory of God and the salvation of souls. We thus imbibe little by little the idea that all our prayers should give glory to God and ask salvation for all people.

The Missal teaches us *how we should pray*. It shows that every prayer should be one of praise, thanksgiving, and petition. Every petition is to be preceded by rendering thanks to God for his past and present favors.

Every prayer is Trinitarian — and the Missal clearly brings this home to us. It is the Spirit who suggests the words to us, Jesus who offers our prayer, and the Father who accepts it. We must pray always in this vein.

The Missal teaches us to avoid particularism, self-centeredness, and one-sidedness. Our personal prayer is seen in perspective with the lives of our co-parishioners, co-members of the Church, and co-members of the human race. We never pray alone — just as we never live alone in this world. What we do always touches others in one way or another.

The Missal indicates *with what qualities we should pray*. We should pray with *devotion* — that is, from the heart and without willful distractions. *Humility* should be another mark of our prayer — that is, we should acknowledge our sinfulness and our need for help.

Our prayer should be offered with *resignation* — that is, we should leave it to God's will as to when and how he will hear us. At the same time, it should be *confident* — that is, it should be uttered with complete trust that God will hear us.

The Missal tells us we should pray with *perseverance* — that is, we should never give up, never stop praying. Jesus said, "In your perseverance you will secure your lives [that is, save your souls]" (Luke 21:19).

Finally, as will be shown graphically below, the Missal provides *content* for our prayer. It contains hundreds of prayers on countless subjects — all based on the language and spirit of God's Word in the Bible. It enables us to pray with the Church by giving us model prayers to use in many life situations. Many consider them to have been inspired by the Holy Spirit, and they form an inexhaustible source of genuine piety for all Christians.

Makeup of the Missal

Before going any further, it may be well to provide a look at the makeup of a Missal. The following outlines show the sequence of the parts of the Mass (as well as whether they are Proper or Ordinary; all unlabeled parts are Ordinary) and the sequence of the liturgical feasts and seasons.

OUTLINE OF THE PARTS OF MASS

INTRODUCTORY RITES

Entrance Antiphon (Proper)
Greeting
Penitential Rite
Kyrie
Gloria
Opening Prayer (Proper)

LITURGY OF THE WORD

> First Reading (Proper)
>   (Old or New Testament except Gospel)
> Responsorial Psalm (Proper)
> Second Reading (Proper)
>   (New Testament except Gospel)
> Gospel (Proper)
> Alleluia or Gospel Acclamation (Proper)
> Homily
>   (Composed for individual celebration)
> Profession of Faith (Nicene Creed)
> General Intercessions (Prayer of the Faithful)
>   (Composed for individual celebration)

LITURGY OF THE EUCHARIST

> *Preparation of the Gifts*
> Offertory Song
> Offering of Gifts and Collection
> Preparation of the Gifts
> Invitation to Prayer
> Prayer over the Gifts (Proper)

> *Eucharistic Prayer*
> Introductory Dialogue
> Preface
> Holy, Holy, Holy
> Eucharistic Prayer
>   No. 1, 2, 3, or 4
>   Children 1, 2, or 3
>   Reconciliation 1 or 2
>   (Every Eucharistic Prayer includes:
>   Memorial Acclamation and Great Amen)

Communion Rite
> Our Father
> Sign of Peace
> Breaking of Bread
> Prayers before Communion
> Reception of Communion
> Communion Antiphon (Proper)
> Silence after Communion
> Prayer after Communion (Proper)

CONCLUDING RITE

> Blessing
> Dismissal

Mass may be celebrated every day, but it is prescribed only on Sundays and Holydays of Obligation: Solemnity of Mary, Mother of God (January 1); Ascension Thursday (40 days after Easter); Assumption of Mary (August 15); All Saints Day (November 1); Immaculate Conception (December 8); Nativity of Jesus (Christmas, December 25). Here is an outline of the Liturgical Year.

OUTLINE OF THE LITURGICAL YEAR

Nov./Dec.	*Advent Season* (4 Sundays before Christmas) *We prepare for the coming of Jesus, who is here and yet to come.*
Dec. 25	Christmas (Birth of Jesus)
Dec./Jan.	*Christmas Season* *We celebrate the gift of our Father's love: Jesus is our brother and our Lord.* Feast of the Holy Family (Sunday after Christmas) Feast of the Epiphany (2nd Sunday after Christmas) (Jesus shows himself to the world)

Jan./Feb.	*Ordinary Time* (between 5 and 9 weeks)
	With Jesus we enter into the work of his Body, the Church.
Feb./Mar.	**Lenten Season**
	We do penance and root out our faults so we may rise with Christ as new persons at Easter.
	Ash Wednesday (40 days before Easter)
	5 Sundays
	Palm Sunday (Christ's Solemn Entry into Jerusalem)
Mar./Apr.	Holy Week culminating in Christ's Resurrection on Easter
	Easter Season (5 Sundays)
	Sharing in the new life of Christ, we are filled with his Spirit.
A Thursday in May	Ascension (40 days after Easter)
	7th Sunday of Easter
May / June	Pentecost (50 days after Easter, sending of the Spirit)
May / June to Nov./Dec.	*Ordinary Time* (continuation of the preceding season between Epiphany and Lent, this season counts 33 or 34 Sundays in all)
	Guided by the Spirit of Jesus, we build the kingdom of God by our lives.
	Feast of Christ the King (Last Sunday of the Liturgical Year)

This calendar is set up based on the fixed feast of Christmas (December 25) and the movable date of Easter: the First Council of Nicaea determined that this feast was to be celebrated on the Sunday after the first full moon of the Spring equinox; Easter can therefore occur anywhere between March 22 and April 25.

On the other days of the year various other feasts are

celebrated, for example, the Annunciation on March 25; there are also feasts of the principal saints assigned to the date of their death — their birth to heavenly glory.

As mentioned already, there is a Proper and an Ordinary. In a complete Missal (both Sunday and Weekday), there are the following sections:

ORDINARY

Contains the invariable parts of the Mass, with selected options

PROPER

Contains the texts that are proper to certain celebrations

Proper of the Season
Contains the feasts of the liturgical calendar mentioned above

Proper of the Saints
Contains the feasts of the saints (some have complete special formularies; others have only one or two proper texts)

Common of the Saints
Contains the complete formulary to celebrate Masses in honor of the saints pertaining to a certain category and which do not have special texts: martyr, virgin, doctor of the Church, pastor, etc.

Ritual Masses
Contains the Masses for the sacramental rites: marriage, funeral, etc.

Votive Masses
Contains the texts for Masses celebrated to petition God for the unity of Christians, peace, etc.

The Sunday Missal contains only the Masses that may occur on Sundays and is very easy to use. Once a person has mastered its use, he or she can come to know how to use the Weekday Missal!

Praying with the Words of the Eucharist

With the aid of a Missal, you can now take advantage of the prayers found in the Eucharist. On almost every page there is a prayer that can be used in any life situation.

Are you seeking God's continual blessings? The 16th Sunday in Ordinary Time will provide a beautiful choice of words and themes for your consideration (Alternative Opening Prayer):

> Father,
> let the gift of your life
> continue to grow in us,
> drawing us from death to faith, hope, and love.
> Keep us alive in Christ Jesus.
> Keep us watchful in prayer
> and true to his teaching
> till your glory is revealed in us.
> Grant this through Christ our Lord.

Are you thinking of repentance? The sentiments in the Alternative Opening Prayer of the 13th Sunday in Ordinary Time are perfect for you:

> Father in heaven,
> the light of Jesus
> has scattered the darkness of hatred and sin.
> Called to that light

we ask for your guidance.
Form our lives in your truth, our hearts in your love.
We ask this through Christ our Lord.

Are you overwhelmed by the evils in this world? Find
strength in the Church's vision of the world set forth in the
Alternative Opening Prayer for the 17th Sunday in Ordinary
Time:

God our Father,
open our eyes to see your hand at work
in the splendor of creation,
in the beauty of human life.
Touched by your hand our world is holy.
Help us to cherish the gifts that surround us,
to share your blessings with our brothers and sisters,
and to experience the joy of life in your presence.
We ask this through Christ our Lord.

Are you searching for a prayer for those out of work and
for those who toil at inhumane jobs? The Votive Mass for the
Blessings of Human Labor has the right prayer for you (Opening Prayer):

God our Father,
by the labor of [human beings] you govern and guide
    to perfection
the work of creation.
Hear the prayers of your people
And give all [persons] work that enhances their
    human dignity
and draws them to each other
in the service of their brothers [and sisters].
We ask this through Christ our Lord.

Are you suffering beneath the weight of the evil that has overtaken you or one of your loved ones? Try praying with the Alternative Opening Prayer of the 2nd Sunday in Ordinary Time:

> Almighty and ever-present Father,
> your watchful care reaches from end to end
> and orders all things with such power
> that even the tensions and the tragedies of sin
> cannot frustrate your loving plans.
> Help us to embrace your will,
> give us the strength to follow your call,
> so that your truth may live in our hearts
> and reflect peace to those who believe in your love.
> We ask this in the name of Jesus the Lord.

Are you in need of a prayer to overcome discouragement? The Alternative Opening Prayer for the 31st Sunday in Ordinary Time is perfect for you:

> Father in heaven, God of power and Lord of mercy,
> from whose fullness we have received,
> direct our steps in our everyday efforts.
> May the changing moods of the human heart
> and the limits which our failings impose on hope
> never blind us to you, source of every good.
> Faith gives us the promise of peace
> and makes known the demands of love.
> Remove the selfishness that blurs the vision of faith.
> Grant this through Christ our Lord.

In this age which looks upon the world as a global village, are you seeking a prayer that captures this spirit while asking for the progress of peoples? The Opening Prayer of the Mass for the Progress of Peoples fills the bill:

Father,
you have given all peoples one common origin,
and your will is to gather them as one family
    in yourself.
Fill the hearts of all [human beings] with the fire
    of your love
and the desire to ensure justice for all their
    brothers and sisters.
By sharing the good things you give us
may we secure justice and equality for every
    human being,
an end to all division,
and a human society built on love and peace.
We ask this through Christ our Lord.

Perhaps you are looking for a special prayer to the Holy
Spirit, something to show his power and role in our lives. The
Sequence for the Mass of Pentecost is just what you need:

Come, Holy Spirit, come!
And from your celestial home
shed a ray of light divine!

Come, Father of the poor!
Come, source of all our store!
Come, within our bosoms shine!

You, of comforters the best;
you, the soul's most welcome guest;
sweet refreshment here;

in our labor, rest most sweet;
grateful coolness in the heat;
solace in the midst of woe.

O most blessed Light divine,
shine within these hearts of yours,
and our inmost being fill!

Where you are not [we have] naught,
nothing good in deed or thought,
nothing free from taint of ill.

Heal our wounds, our strength renew;
on our dryness pour your dew;
wash the stains of guilt away:

bend the stubborn heart and will;
melt the frozen, warm the chill;
guide the steps that go astray.

On the faithful, who adore
and confess you, evermore
in your sev'nfold gift descend;

give them virtue's sure reward;
give them your salvation, Lord;
give them joys that never end.
Amen. Alleluia.

Are you desirous of finding the right words to thank God for his tremendous gift of the Eucharist? The Preface for the Feast of the Body and Blood of Christ is perfect:

Father, all-powerful and ever-living God,
we do well always and everywhere to give you thanks
through Jesus Christ our Lord.

At the last supper,
as he sat at table with his apostles,
he offered himself to you as the spotless lamb,
the acceptable gift that gives you perfect praise.
Christ has given us this memorial of his passion
to bring us its saving power until the end of time.

In this great sacrament you feed your people
and strengthen them in holiness,
so that the family of mankind

may come to walk in the light of one faith,
in one communion of love.
We come then to this wonderful sacrament
to be fed at your table
and grow into the likeness of the risen Christ.

Earth unites with heaven
to sing the new song of creation
as we adore and praise you for ever:

Holy, holy, holy Lord, God of power and might,
heaven and earth are full of your glory.
Hosanna in the highest.
Blessed is he who comes in the name of the Lord.
Hosanna in the highest.

We could go on and on, indicating texts. For every mood, for every need, for every mentality, there is a prayer. Every day there is a Responsorial Psalm that makes apt prayer material for us. The Prefaces are unique in their beauty and doctrine. The Sequences combine poetry and prayer. The Opening Prayers are always there for our use.

All we need do is leaf through a Missal. On every page a golden treasury of prayers lies waiting for our use. We simply have to choose one and pray!

6

PRAYING
THE SACRAMENTS

The word *sacrament* generally refers to the intervention of God in history manifesting his will. The Church speaks of the "sacraments of nature" and the "sacraments of the Old Testament," Christ as the "sacrament of God" and the Church as the "sacrament of salvation."

When it is applied to the seven sacraments of the New Covenant, the word has a special meaning. It means "an outward sign instituted by Christ to give grace." Thus, the sacraments may be termed acts of Christ who personally sanctifies each individual through them.

They are also acts of the Church, which continues the priestly office of Christ in the world. She carries out in the world the purpose of the Incarnation.

Christ's saving acts took place once for all in history. They obtained grace and glory for all human beings. The sacraments bring that grace to individuals and give that glory as a pledge to come. Indeed, the sacraments are the chief vehicles through which grace is communicated to us.

In the words of Vatican II, "the purpose of the sacraments

is to sanctify human beings, to build up the Body of Christ, and finally to give worship to God; because they are signs, they also instruct. They do indeed impart grace, but, in addition, the very act of celebrating them most effectively disposes the faithful to receive this grace in a fruitful manner" (*Constitution on the Sacred Liturgy*, no. 59).

Thus, the sacraments have been called "living encounters with Christ." They put us in touch with the Risen Jesus and enable us to receive his saving grace through the power of the Holy Spirit. They thereby provide excellent opportunities for us to enrich our prayer life — for they are prayers in the best sense of the word.

Every celebration of the sacraments is a prayer of Christ and a cause of prayer for us. Through the sacraments (and the sacramentals, their extensions and radiations), we can extend the Eucharistic worship into all space, time, and matter. We can sanctify each and every day. We can transform our lives and the whole world.

> For well-disposed members of the faithful, the liturgy of the sacraments and sacramentals sanctifies almost every event of their lives with the divine grace that flows from the Paschal Mystery of the passion, death, and resurrection of Christ. From this source all sacraments and sacramentals draw their power. There is scarcely any proper use of material things that cannot thus be directed toward the sanctification of human beings and the praise of God (*Constitution on the Sacred Liturgy*, no. 61).

Praying the sacraments with the right dispositions elevates us above ourselves and above the whole natural order to the divine sphere. The sacraments infuse new life into us that we may live truly for God. Not only do they infuse that life, but they conserve and augment it.

Christ, the Sacrament of the Encounter with God

Every communication between human beings takes place through gestures, words, and actions. We can open up to others in order to encounter them only by using concrete things or actions. But these are ambiguous for the most part. This is the reason for words. They explain the actions performed and help people understand the depth of the gesture made.

God has communicated himself to us through gestures, actions, and words that we call sacraments. They are gestures of God through the Spirit. God's great sacramental gesture was to become a human being. Hence, Christ is the first and the true sacrament. He is the efficacious sign that human beings can be divinized — share God's life.

In the Incarnation, in Jesus of Nazareth, a human nature is elevated to the divine dignity. This took place not for Jesus alone — for he is the Word of God from eternity and for all eternity — but for us as well. Christ is the sign, the type, the model of the divine filiation to which God wants to elevate all human beings.

It is absolutely true that Christ is God and that everything he did as man is an act of the Son of God and an act of God. However, we must not imagine that Christ's divinity shone visibly through his body. Without faith his contemporaries saw him only as a man.

In order for them to encounter Jesus as God-Man, they required faith. They required the eyes of faith and a heart open to God, capable of reading his human actions as *signs of God*.

Not even the followers of Christ saw God all at once in our Lord's words and behavior. Only gradually was the mystery of his person made known to them — the mystery of God's presence and compassion.

This is what Jesus indicated in his reply to Philip who asked him to show the Father to his disciples: "Have I been with you for so long a time and you still do not know me, Philip? Whoever has seen me has seen the Father" (John 14:8-9).

In time, the disciples and then the Church came to realize that the love of the Man Jesus is in effect the human incarnation of God's redeeming love. It is a coming of God's love in visible form. Thus, because the human actions of Christ are actions of God, they possess a divine power of salvation. They are salvific — causes of grace and salvation.

And since this divine form appears to human beings under an earthly and visible form, the saving actions of Jesus are *sacramental*. For a sacrament, as we have seen, symbolizes a divine manifestation and gift of salvation — and through a very palpable form, which concretizes the gift.

All the actions of Jesus during his earthly life are ultimately intended to give life — eternal life. This is the message of the Resurrection that he worked: "I am the resurrection and the life" (John 11:25).

These actions will perdure until the end of the world. For Christ, the sacrament of our encounter with God, is still with us. He works those same actions for us through the sacraments of the Church.

The sacraments rightly celebrated bring the hope of the Church to the world. They are advance signs of the completion of the world in Jesus Christ. Thus, just as the Incarnate Christ was the visage of the Father, so the Church is the visage of the risen and ascended Christ for all people on earth. She is the efficacious sign, the sacrament, that renders him present to the world.

Signs of Faith

The sacraments are efficacious signs of the Covenant of God with human beings. They both reveal it and realize it at the same time. In the celebration of the sacraments, the risen Jesus is really present. Through actions and words, he communicates to us the intention of salvation that he pursues in the world and that he is in the process of achieving in us here and now.

He also indicates the dispositions and life attitude that he expects from us in the Covenant that he proposes to us in each sacrament. He helps us *with power*. This is the sacramental grace that flows from each sacrament.

None of this is visible; it must be inferred; it depends on faith. First the faith of the Church. Without the faith of the Church, there is no sacrament. This is what is known as the intention of the minister *to do what the Church wants* in any sacrament — which is in turn what Christ wants.

Such faith is what makes the sacraments efficacious by themselves, by the very power of their positing. So long as this faith is present, the sacraments are really acts of Christ who comes to encounter us. Nothing is lacking from his part.

However, the liturgy is a dialogue; it cannot be one-sided. Another faith is needed to make the sacraments fulfill their effect in people — the faith of the recipients. Without faith the sacraments are useless to those who receive them. And this faith is essentially faith in Christ the Redeemer — an explicit faith in Jesus Christ who died and rose for the salvation of all human beings.

In the final analysis, the sacraments must be celebrated *in spirit and in truth*. *In spirit* means not a disembodied worship but a worship whose ceremonies have a meaning, inspire devotion, suggest the mystery of God, elevate the soul, and give it a sense of consecration.

In truth means a true preaching of the Gospel through the sacraments. The external expressions of the sacraments are regulated logically and in a way that imparts the real meaning of the rite to all present.

Personal Encounters with Christ

In every sacrament, the Jesus who touches us — who pardons, heals, invests us with his priesthood, or with his love — is always the Jesus of the Paschal Mystery, the Jesus eternally established in what is the culminating part of his life and his right to glory: the event of his death and resurrection.

Every sacrament plunges us *spiritually but really* into the very act of Jesus dying to sin and rising to new life. Hence, each sacrament — not only the Eucharist — is a memorial of the death and resurrection of Christ.

As we have seen, when we pray the sacraments Jesus is really present to us today. This is a *personal presence*. We meet Jesus, we become transformed in him, and we are conformed to him in the manner proper to each sacrament.

Accordingly, we must prepare to encounter him corporally but symbolically with faith and love:

1) in the Scripture proclaimed and the Word announced: "Whoever listens to you listens to me" (Luke 10:16);

2) in the sole fact of gathering together in his Church to celebrate him: "Where two or three are gathered together in my name, there am I in the midst of them" (Matthew 18:20);

3) in the sacrament of baptism: "Go, therefore, and make disciples of all nations, baptizing them in the name of the Father, and of the Son, and of the Holy Spirit" (Matthew 28:19);

4) in the sacrament of the Eucharist: "Take and eat. . . . Drink from it, all of you. . . . Do this in memory of me" (Matthew 26:26; Luke 22:19);

5) in the fraternal correction and reconciliation in the community: "Whatever you loose on earth shall be loosed in heaven" (Matthew 18:18); "Receive the Holy Spirit.

Whose sins you forgive are forgiven them" (John 20:22-23);
6) and in the other sacraments.

Only the eyes of faith can discern the true presence of Jesus in this world. The Lord awaits us, but our human eyes are prevented from seeing him. It takes our entire person to encounter Christ in this world. The sacraments are our indicators to Christ. They facilitate our encounter with him.

We must listen with openness to his Word and participate wholeheartedly in the sacramental Action. Through that Word and that Action, the Lord himself draws near us, speaks to us, and becomes united with us. In other words, we must be ready to meet Christ on his terms, not ours. For it is not we who go out to meet Christ but he who comes to meet us.

In this encounter we must be prepared to be transformed. When God meets human beings, they are inevitably changed for the better. They put on a new life. In order to meet Christ we must accept the law of the Paschal Mystery in our life — the law of life through death.

Each sacrament plunges the Paschal Mystery into the realities of our individual lives. It demands that we be freely disposed to embrace the *conversion* that alone gives new life. We must, in short, seek God more than self: "Whoever finds his life will lose it, and whoever loses his life [does not seek self] for my sake will find it" (Matthew 10:39).

The practical sign of this acceptance is that our encounter with Christ in any sacrament goes on to bear fruit in our earthly lives — that it makes us better witnesses to Christ before others.

The important thing in the reception of each sacrament is to let ourselves be "worked on" by it: to get our faith into it, to really thirst for it, to listen to it, to enter into it with the best possible dispositions — and then to wait, letting the sacramental grace flow into our lives.

Praying the Sacraments

In a sense, it is not as easy to pray the sacraments as we pray the Eucharist. The most obvious reason is because we do not receive the sacraments as often as we participate at Mass.

At baptism most of us do not know what is going on. Our participation is done by our godparents, who take our place. Upon reaching adulthood, we then endorse this reception of baptism. We assent to what has been done in our name. A good way to do this is by renewing the baptismal promises made for us.

We receive confirmation only once — usually at the beginning of teenagehood. At this time, we hardly know what liturgy is and what it means to us. Our participation is at best imperfect. Praying this sacrament is once again not what it would be if we received it at an adult age. We can merely meditate upon its effects and strive to implement this sacrament more in our lives.

We receive marriage or holy orders once also (except that, after the death of a spouse, we can marry again). We can pray these two sacraments fully because we receive them as adults. We can utilize all the points made above to insure that our reception will be full, conscious, and active.

Usually, we receive the anointing of the sick once also (although we may receive it any number of times if there is reason for it). This sacrament, too, lends itself to real participation on our part. We can enter into it with understanding, faith, and total openness.

The only two sacraments that we receive as often as we wish and can pray with complete effectiveness are the Eucharist and penance. We have already dealt with praying the Eucharist. Here we might give a few pointers on praying the sacrament of penance.

By its very nature the sacrament of penance is conducive

to prayer. It is prayer that will enable us to bring forth in our lives signs of repentance and reconciliation and to enter into the Paschal Mystery. We prepare for the reception of the sacrament by prayer and an examination of conscience. We pray for the grace of true contrition and worthy reception of the sacrament.

When we begin the new rite, it is by prayerfully listening and responding to a text of the Word of God proclaimed by the priest. We then say a prayer of contrition. After confessing our sins, we receive absolution and give praise to God in union with the priest. Indeed, this may be the easiest sacrament for us to pray!

However, there is another sense in which it is easy for us to pray the sacraments. We can pray them not only in the liturgical celebration but also in their prolonged celebration in our lives.

The sacraments are not intended to be static moments in our lives. They are in a sense all of our lives. At the moment of liturgical celebration, everything is placed as if in a germ or a seed, but it must be lived out in a lifetime.

Each sacrament possesses its own value and its particular function. Certainly, it imparts the divine life substantially and identically — but with modifications proper to each sacrament. Each of them places its own proper stamp on the divine life it gives us.

This is the so-called sacramental grace, the particular aspect that — with the life of Christ given by each sacrament — is communicated to us and that consequently calls for an accounting from us. Each sacrament assimilates us to some aspect of the personality of Christ the Redeemer.

Each of us must seek to discover the riches of a sacrament received — even one received in the distant past. In God's plan the reality once received must continue to nourish and characterize our new life. If we cooperate with the sacramental grace — if we "pray" the sacraments well in this fashion — we will realize ourselves fully and be forever "of the Lord, with the Lord, and in the Lord."

Cooperating with Sacramental Grace

Each of the sacraments is both an encounter and a prayer. It is an encounter with Christ whose hand touches us through the Church's rite. It is also an encounter with the Father in a particularly effective prayer "through Jesus Christ his Son, our Lord." It is a prayer that assimilates us to that same Son. The sacrament makes us adopted children of God, reconciled with God, confirmed in our new life, healed of all evil, united in God's love, and filled with the Holy Spirit.

The Holy Spirit is the first Gift of baptism and confirmation; he is also the gift of every sacrament received with faith. The "grace" of the sacrament is not something but Someone. It is the Spirit — who intensifies his presence in us, his activity, his light, his tenderness, and his prayer.

Whenever baptism, confirmation, holy orders, or marriage establishes us in a new permanent state of filial life, it opens up in us a new and inexhaustible source of grace. Living these states and drinking from their sources of grace is nothing more than prayer: "Rejoice always. Pray without ceasing. In all circumstances give thanks, for this is the will of God for you in Christ Jesus. Do not quench the Spirit" (1 Thessalonians 5:16-19).

In *baptism* Christ makes us like himself insofar as he is the Son of the Father, and he gives us the spirit of this sonship. By cooperating with the grace of the sacrament, we are to become ever more active children of God in the Son of God.

In *confirmation* Christ makes us like himself insofar as he is the herald and founder of the kingdom of God, and he communicates to us in germ his missionary and apostolic spirit. By cooperating with the grace of the sacrament, we are to become ever more mature witnesses for him to the world, even ready to shed our blood if need be after his example and that of the martyrs.

In the *Eucharist* Christ makes us like himself insofar as he is Love, and he gives us the spirit of his priesthood and victimhood. By cooperating with the grace of the sacrament, we are to become even more united with him, "the person for others beyond compare." We are to love not for ourselves but in solidarity with and for others.

In *penance* Christ makes us like himself insofar as he is the victim of expiation for the sins of the world, and he gives us his spirit of penance. By cooperating with the grace of the sacrament, we are to pray for those who do not pray and to make reparation for those who do not make reparation.

In *marriage* Christ makes us like himself insofar as he is the Spouse of the Church, and he gives us his spirit of loving union. By cooperating with the grace of the sacrament, spouses are to love one another as Christ loves the Church.

In *holy orders* Christ makes us like himself insofar as he is the eternal high priest, and he gives us the spirit of self-offering that he carried out in his priesthood. By cooperating with the grace of the sacrament, priests are to utilize their prophetic, liturgical, and pastoral function to show forth the love of the Father for the glory of God and the salvation of the world.

In the *anointing of the sick* Christ makes us like himself insofar as he is the wonderworker and healer as well as the Man of Sorrows, and he gives us the spirit in which he accepted the Cross. By cooperating with the grace of the sacrament, we are to transform earthly trials into means of purification, tears into spiritual pearls, thorns into mystical roses, and ultimately death into eternal life.

If we follow these little emphases, we will be praying the sacraments with our whole lives. We will also be living them to the fullest extent of our ability.

In this way we will be refashioned ever more day by day into the image and likeness of Christ. We will be configured to him and transfigured in him to the point that we can repeat: "I live, no longer I, but Christ lives in me" (Galatians 2:20).

7

PRAYING
WITH THE SACRAMENTS

As was the case with praying the sacraments discussed in the previous chapter, praying *with* the sacraments also takes a bit different tack from praying with the Eucharist. Since the prayers found in each sacramental rite are directed to a particular end, they cannot be used as freely as the prayers in the Eucharist.

However, we can use the prayers of each sacrament to reinforce the grace of the sacrament, as explained in Chapter 6. We can pray to foster the ends of the sacrament in our lives.

In a sense, the sacraments also enable us to pray because three of them impart a special *character* to us. This special character is connected with the priesthood of Christ, which governs all prayer.

The sacraments of baptism, confirmation, and holy orders impart an unction produced in our souls by God through the Holy Spirit. It indicates that we belong to God forever and that we are the property of Christ so as to share in his fundamental prerogatives.

The sacramental character gives us a share in Christ's fundamental prerogative of being a high priest, which he has imparted to the Church making it a royal priesthood and a holy people of God. The Church is destined to give the Father all the honor and glory that sin has attempted to take away from him and to bring complete salvation and true freedom to all people and all things.

A first share in this priesthood of Christ is given us by baptism. We receive the "priesthood of the faithful." Through it we join in the offering of the Eucharist. We likewise express that priesthood in receiving the sacraments, in *prayer* and thanksgiving, in the witness of a holy life, and in self-denial and active charity.

A second share in this priesthood is given by the character in confirmation. We acquire the disposition to carry out the prophetic and evangelical function that the Church is called to exercise. This does not do away with or impede the canonical mission of those deputed to carry it out as priests.

An even more intense share in this priesthood is given by the character of holy orders. It configures priests to Christ the priest (in accord with the various grades: bishops, priests, or deacons) and makes them guides, pastors, and heads of the community of believers.

These two priesthoods — the priesthood of the faithful and the ministerial priesthood — differ from one another not only in degree but also in essence. Yet they have in common the quality that both empower us to *pray as Christians* (a characteristic already mentioned in Chapter 1). If we are enabled to pray *with* the sacraments, for instance, it is only because we possess the characters that inspire our prayer, facilitate our prayer, and perfect our prayer.

Baptism

Baptism makes us children of God sanctified by the Spirit, unites us with Jesus in his death and resurrection, cleanses us from sin (both original and personal), and welcomes us into the community of the Church. It relates us permanently to God in a relationship that can never be erased and joins us to the priestly, prophetic, and kingly works of Christ.

One of the best ways to pray *with* this sacrament is to renew the baptismal promises made in our name when we received it. This will enable us to keep the grace of the sacrament working and live the sacrament explicitly as well as implicitly.

The renewal is found in the Easter Vigil and essentially reproduces the text used at baptism.

> Do you reject Satan?
> I do.
> And all his works?
> I do.
> And all his empty promises?
> I do.

OR

> Do you reject sin, so as to live in the freedom of
>   God's children?
> I do.
> Do you reject the glamor of evil, and refuse to be
>   mastered by sin?
> I do.
> Do you reject Satan, father of sin and prince of
>   darkness?
> I do.
>
> Do you believe in God, the Father almighty, creator
>   of heaven and earth?
> I do.

Do you believe in Jesus Christ, his only Son, our Lord,
who was born of the Virgin Mary,
was crucified, died, and was buried,
rose from the dead,
and is now seated at the right hand of the Father?
I do.

Do you believe in the Holy Spirit,
the holy Catholic Church, the communion of saints,
the forgiveness of sins, the resurrection of the body,
and life everlasting?
I do.

God, the all-powerful Father of our Lord Jesus Christ,
[you have] given us a new birth by water and the
    Holy Spirit,
and forgiven our sins.
. . . Keep us faithful to our Lord Jesus Christ
    for ever and ever.

Confirmation

Through the sacrament of confirmation, Jesus sends the
Holy Spirit once more to us with new grace and new strength
to lead the Christian life. We are empowered to live in the
world as a witness of Christ and as a helper of other human
beings.

Thus, we have the task of bringing Jesus, his example,
his way of life, and his Church to others. The strength of the
grace of the Holy Spirit will help us each to fulfill our
apostolate if we but show some effort and ask his help in
prayer. In this respect the prayers below are perfect for our
use.

All-powerful God, Father of our Lord Jesus Christ,
by water and the Holy Spirit
you freed [us] from sin
and gave [us] new life.
Send your Holy Spirit upon [us]
to be [our] Helper and Guide.
Give [us] the spirit of wisdom and understanding,
the spirit of right judgment and courage,
the spirit of knowledge and reverence.
Fill [us] with the spirit of wonder and awe in your
    presence.
We ask this through Christ our Lord.

OR

God our Father
made [us] his children by water and the Holy Spirit:
may he bless [us]
and watch over [us] with his fatherly love.

Jesus Christ the Son of God
promised that the Spirit of truth
would be with his Church for ever:
may he bless [us] and give [us] courage
in professing the true faith.

The Holy Spirit
came down upon the disciples
and set their hearts on fire with love:
may he bless [us],
keep [us] one in faith and love
and bring [us] to the joy of God's kingdom.

Penance

Through the sacrament of penance, Jesus the Good
Shepherd forgives our sins and sends his Holy Spirit once more
to our soul to help us lead the Christian life and to grow

spiritually. Thus, penance not only forgives sin but also develops virtues in us that make us more Christlike.

Penance reminds us of God's great love for us. His love must inspire us to greater love for him. Through the grace of the sacrament our love will never flag if we do not neglect to pray.

This sacrament also increases our hope. We realize that even though we are sinners we can obtain from God the help we need to reach heaven. Our prayer will reinforce this hope.

Faith is also strengthened in the sacrament of penance because like every sacrament penance demands the exercise of faith. We believe that Christ instituted this sacrament for the forgiveness of our sins and for our reconciliation with God and his people. Our prayer will increase our faith.

The following two prayers from the rite can help us live this sacrament to the full.

>Almighty and merciful God,
>you have brought us together in the name of your Son
>to receive your mercy and grace in our time of need.
>Open our eyes to see the evil we have done.
>Touch our hearts and convert us to yourself.
>
>Where sin has divided and scattered,
>may your love make one again;
>where sin has brought weakness,
>may your power heal and strengthen;
>where sin has brought death,
>may your Spirit raise to new life.
>
>Give us a new heart to love you,
>so that our lives may reflect the image of your Son.
>May the world see the glory of Christ
>revealed in your Church,
>and come to know
>that he is the one whom you have sent,
>Jesus Christ, your Son, our Lord.

OR

Lord God,
creator and ruler of your kingdom of light,
in your great love for this world
you gave up your only Son
for our salvation.
His cross has redeemed us,
his death has given us life,
his resurrection has raised us to glory.
Through him we ask you
to be always present among your family.
Teach us to be reverent in the presence of your glory;
fill our hearts with faith,
our days with good works,
our lives with your love;
may your truth be on our lips
and your wisdom in all our actions,
that we may receive the reward of everlasting life.
We ask this through Christ our Lord.

Marriage

In the sacrament of marriage, Christ comes to man and wife to live with them, to give them his grace, and to help them fulfill their rights and duties to God, to each other, and to their children faithfully until death. The Holy Spirit breathes God's own love into the love between husband and wife so that as they selflessly share their life in God each becomes a minister of grace to the other.

As a result the couple's many acts of self-giving not only strengthen their life together but also cause them to grow in the life of God. He incorporates them as husband and wife in

Christ and gives them the means by which they can adjust to one another.

The following prayers can be of help in bringing about the grace of the sacrament throughout the married life of the spouses.

Father,
keep us always true to your commandments.
Keep [us] faithful in marriage
and let [us] be living examples of Christian life.
Give [us] the strength which comes from the gospel
so that [we] may be witnesses of Christ to others.
Bless [us] with children
and help us to be good parents.
May [we] live to see [our] children's children.
And after a happy old age,
grant [us] fullness of life with the saints
in the kingdom of heaven.
We ask this through Christ our Lord.

OR

May almighty God,
with his Word of blessing,
unite [our] hearts in the never-ending bond of pure love.

May [our] children bring [us] happiness,
and may [our] generous love for them
be returned to us, many times over.

May the peace of Christ live always
in [our] hearts and in [our] home.
May [we] have friends to stand by [us],
both in joy and in sorrow.
May [we] be ready and willing to help and comfort
all who come to [us] in need.

And may the blessings promised to the compassionate
be [ours] in abundance.

May [we] find happiness and satisfaction
in our work.

May daily problems never cause [us] undue anxiety
nor the desire for earthly possessions dominate [our]
    lives.

But may [our] heart's first desire be always
the good things waiting for [us] in the life of heaven.

May the Lord bless [us] with many happy years
    together,
so that [we] may enjoy the rewards of a good life.

And after [we] have served him loyally in his
    kingdom on earth,
may he welcome [us] to his eternal kingdom in heaven.

Holy Orders

In the sacrament of holy orders, Christ bestows a permanent charism or grace of the Holy Spirit enabling the recipients
to guide and shepherd the faith community, proclaim and
explain the Gospel, and guide and sanctify God's people.

Bishops, priests, and deacons, who are the recipients of
this sacrament, can make use of the prayers of the rite to
strengthen their ministerial spirit and implement the grace of
the sacramental character throughout their lives. Professed
religious can also use the prayers of their profession in the
same way — even though they do not receive a sacrament. And
the laity can utilize such prayers to pray for their priests.

The following prayers can be prayed by all three classes
of people just mentioned — simply by changing the pronouns
and making other modifications as needed.

(For Bishops)

Father, you know all hearts.
You have chosen your servant for the office of bishop.
May he be a shepherd to your holy flock,
and a high priest blameless in your sight,
ministering to you night and day;
may he always gain the blessing of your favor
and offer the gifts of your holy Church.
Through the Spirit who gives the grace of high priesthood
grant him the power
to forgive sins as you have commanded,
to assign ministries as you have decreed,
and to loose every bond by the authority which you
    gave to your apostles.
May he be pleasing to you by his gentleness and
    purity of heart,
presenting a fragrant offering to you,
through Jesus Christ, your Son,
through whom glory and power are yours
with the Holy Spirit
in your holy Church,
now and for ever.

(For Priests)

Almighty Father,
[you granted] to these servants of yours
the dignity of the priesthood.
Renew within them the Spirit of holiness.
As co-workers with the order of bishops
may they be faithful to the ministry
that they [have received] from you, Lord God,
and be to others a model of right conduct.

May they be faithful in working with the order of bishops,
so that the words of the Gospel may reach the ends of
    the earth,
and the family of nations,
made one in Christ,
may become God's one, holy people.
We ask this through Christ our Lord.

(*For Deacons*)

Lord,
send forth upon them the Holy Spirit,
that they may be strengthened
by the gift of your sevenfold grace
to carry out faithfully the work of the ministry.

May they excel in every virtue:
in love that is sincere,
in concern for the sick and the poor,
in unassuming authority,
in self-discipline,
and in holiness of life.

May their conduct exemplify your commandments,
and lead your people to imitate their purity of life.
May they remain strong and steadfast in Christ,
giving to the world the witness of a pure conscience.
May they in this life imitate your Son,
who came, not to be served but to serve,
and one day reign with him in heaven.
We ask this through Christ our Lord.

(*For Religious*)

Through the gift of your Spirit, Lord,
give them modesty with right judgment,

kindness with true wisdom,
gentleness with strength of character,
freedom with the grace of chastity.
Give them the warmth of love,
to love you above all others.
Make their lives deserve our praise,
without seeking to be praised.
May they give you glory
by holiness of action and purity of heart.
May they love you and fear you;
may they love you and serve you.

Be yourself their glory, their joy, their whole desire.
Be their comfort in sorrow,
their wisdom in perplexity,
their protection in the midst of injustice,
their patience in adversity,
their riches in poverty,
their food in fasting,
their remedy in time of sickness.

They have chosen you above all things;
may they find all things in possessing you.
We ask this through Christ our Lord.

Anointing of the Sick

In the sacrament of the anointing of the sick, Christ
comes to the sick. Through the grace of the Holy Spirit, the
whole person is brought to health, trust in God is encouraged,
and strength is given to resist temptations and overcome anxiety about death.

This sacrament also prepares the dying for immediate
entrance into glory. Besides forgiving their sins, Jesus helps

the dying to offer themselves, their lives, and their sufferings
to him with sincere Christian resignation.

We can say the prayers below in times of personal sickness or for the sick and the dying — simply by changing the
pronouns as needed.

(*Personal Sickness*)

Father,
in your love
you gave us Jesus
to help us rise triumphant over grief and pain.
Look on your Child who is sick
and see in [my] sufferings those of your Son.
Grant [me] a share in the strength you granted your Son
that [I] too may be a sign
of your goodness, kindness, and loving care.
We ask this in the name of Jesus the Lord.

(*For the Sick*)

Father,
your Son accepted our sufferings
to teach us the virtue of patience in human illness.
Hear the prayers we offer for our sick [brothers and
    sisters].
May all who suffer pain, illness, or disease
realize that they have been chosen to be saints
and know that they are joined to Christ
in his suffering for the salvation of the world.
We ask this through Christ our Lord.

(*For the Aged*)

All praise and glory are yours, Lord our God,
for you have called us to serve you in love.

Bless all who have grown old in your service
and give [them] strength and courage
to continue to follow Jesus your Son.
We ask this through Christ our Lord.

(For the Dying)

I commend you, my dear [brothers and sisters]
to almighty God,
and entrust you to your Creator.
May you return to him
who formed you from the dust of the earth.
May holy Mary, the angels, and all the saints
come to meet you as you go forth from this life.
May Christ who was crucified for you
bring you freedom and peace.
May Christ who died for you
admit you into his garden of paradise.
May Christ, the true Shepherd,
acknowledge you as one of his flock.
May he forgive all your sins,
and set you among those he has chosen.
May you see your Redeemer face to face,
and enjoy the vision of God for ever.

8

PRAYING
THE SACRAMENTALS

 A s we have seen, Jesus has transformed the world through his death and resurrection. He has made it part of a "sacramental world," so that the effects of the salvation he once accomplished for us *in history* now reach us through the sacramental rites *in mystery*.

The means by which this transformation takes place are the sacraments (which we have already treated) and the sacramentals. Both ultimately derive from Christ — the first from the personal, historical Christ and the latter from the mystical Christ in his Church. Indeed, the sacramentals are extensions and radiations of the sacraments and have the same cause — the passion, death, and resurrection of Christ.

However, the sacramentals differ from the sacraments in three ways. They were not directly instituted by Christ, do not produce grace of themselves, and are not signs of his direct action on our souls. They were instituted by the Church and obtain graces for us indirectly by arousing us to those acts of virtue which draw down God's grace on us.

Thus the Church defines sacramentals as "sacred signs" by which in imitation of the sacraments spiritual effects especially are signified and are obtained by the intercession of the Church (Canon 1166).

The chief benefits obtained by the use of sacramentals are: (1) actual or helping graces; (2) forgiveness of venial sins; (3) remission of temporal punishment due to sin; (4) health of body and material blessings; and (5) protection from evil spirits.

There are literally hundreds of sacramentals and the chief ones are: (1) blessings; (2) exorcisms; and (3) blessed objects of devotion. Some of the most used objects are: ashes, candles, crucifixes, images (of Jesus, Mary, and the saints), medals, palms, rosaries, and scapulars. Others are Church buildings and appurtenances, sacred vessels and vestments, and the Stations of the Cross.

Through the use of the sacramentals in our daily lives and activities we continue the work of the sacraments or prepare for their reception. This is especially true of blessings, which have a direct link to our everyday lives.

The sprinkling of holy water at the beginning of the Sunday Eucharist and the blessing of infants and children are prolongations of the sacrament of baptism. And Benediction of the Blessed Sacrament is a prolongation of the Eucharist.

Blessings of a school, a library, or a typewriter are extensions of the sacrament of confirmation. The Consecration of Virgins is a follow-up of the sacrament of holy orders.

The Confiteor at Mass, the papal blessing at the hour of death, and exorcisms are prolongations of the sacrament of penance. The blessing of the sick and the blessing of oil, medicine, and linens are extensions of the sacrament of the anointing of the sick.

Finally, the blessings of a bridal chamber, of an expectant mother, and of various materials in a home are prolongations of the sacrament of marriage.

Thus, by praying the sacramentals we can extend the

Eucharistic worship into all space, time, and matter. We can sanctify each and every day. We can transform our lives and the whole world.

However, we must remember that sacramentals are not magic formulas. Their effect depends on us. We must use them with true faith and devotion. Only then will they fulfill the purpose for which the Church has given them to us.

As a matter of fact, in ordering the reform of sacramentals, the Second Vatican Council decreed that in their celebration special attention should be given to the full, conscious, and active participation of the people. Therefore, the new sacramentals (as for example the blessings) are so drawn up that they lead to participation on our part.

To pray the sacramentals, then, we need the same kind of participation required for all liturgical services (as already discussed). We should strive to intensify our personal dispositions through faith, for which all things are possible. We should place our assurance in the hope that does not disappoint. Above all, we should be inspired by the love that impels us to keep God's commandments.

If we do our part, the sacramentals will do theirs. They will help us to practice acts of virtue that draw down God's graces on us. They will obtain favors from God through the prayers of the Church offered for us and through the devotion they inspire in us.

They will make us ready to receive sanctifying grace, the life of God. They will also prepare us to receive whatever actual graces God wishes to give us.

Blessings

The celebration of blessings holds a privileged place among all the sacramentals created by the Church for the pastoral benefit of the people of God. As a liturgical action, the celebration leads us to praise God and prepares us for the principal effect of the sacraments. By celebrating a blessing we can also sanctify the various situations and events in our lives.

When we receive a blessing, it is God who is communicating or declaring his own goodness; his ministers bless God by praising him and thanking him and by offering him their reverent worship and service. When we bless others in God's name, we invoke the divine help upon them.

Thus, blessings refer first and foremost to God, whose majesty and goodness they extol. They also involve human beings, whom he governs and in his goodness protects. Further, blessings apply to other created things through which, in their abundance and variety, God blesses us.

Through her blessings, the Church calls us to praise God, encourages us to implore his protection, exhorts us to seek mercy by our holiness of life, and provides us with ways of *praying* that God will grant the favors we ask.

The Church gives glory to God in all things and is particularly intent on showing forth his glory to those who have been or will be reborn through his grace. For us and with us, the Church in celebrating her blessings praises the Lord and implores divine grace at important moments in our lives.

At times the Church also invokes blessings on objects and places connected with human occupations or activities and those related to the blessing or to piety and popular devotions. But such blessings are invoked always with a view to *people* — who use the objects to be blessed and frequent the places to be blessed.

God has given into our use and care the good things he has created, and we are also the recipients of his own wisdom. Thus praying the blessings becomes the means for us to profess that as we make use of what God has created we wish to find him and to love and serve him with fidelity.

Through the guidance of faith, the assurance of hope, and the inspiration of charity, we receive the wisdom to discern the reflection of God's goodness not only in the elements of creation but also in the events of human life. We see all of these as signs of that fatherly providence by which God guides and governs all things.

At all times and in every situation, then, we have an occasion for praising God through Christ in the Holy Spirit. We have an occasion for calling on divine help as well as for giving thanks in all things.

Finally, it is worth noting that laypeople can not only participate in blessings but also celebrate some blessings. For example, parents may bless their children, and their own parents as well as the pets of their household.

It is worthwhile for us to know some of the blessings that are available to us — and to ask our parish priests if a certain event or occasion in our lives is in the line of the Church's blessings.

Some of the many blessings are for: families, married couples, children, engaged couples, a mother before and after childbirth, elderly people, the sick, catechists, pilgrims, and travelers. There are blessings for new buildings, new homes, offices, shops, or factories, means of transportation, tools, animals, and the harvest as well as before and after meals. Finally, there are blessings for objects used in liturgical services such as baptismal fonts, bells, crosses, lecterns, organs, images, and holy water as well as religious articles, rosaries, and scapulars. There are even blessings for any need and occasion.

Sacramental Actions

We also have sacramental actions at our disposal. These are movements of the body that the Church has us use when she honors the Eucharist and administers the sacraments. They including standing, kneeling, folding our hands, bowing, and making the sign of the cross.

Standing is a characteristic human action that indicates the sense of legitimate pride humans have as rational creatures of God. It is also a sign of respect for others. For instance, at Mass we stand at the proclamation of the Gospel to show our respect for Christ who comes to speak his Word to us.

Bowing is a mark of reverence that expresses our submission to God. For example, at Mass we bow during the recitation of the Creed when we mention the Incarnation of the Second Person of the Blessed Trinity.

Kneeling and *genuflecting* are signs of worship as well as signs of intense supplication and humble prayer. Kneeling is also the best means we have for expressing lowliness and humility before God. For example, at Mass we kneel throughout the Eucharistic Prayer showing worship for the Risen Christ who becomes present in the consecrated host and cup as well as our intense union with the prayer being recited in our name by the celebrant.

Folding one's hands, with or without intertwining fingers, indicates readiness to pray and to listen. For example, at Mass after receiving Communion, we fold our hands as we kneel in prayer and union with Jesus.

Possibly the most important sacramental is the *sign of the cross*. We usually begin and end our prayer with this wonderful sign which manifests our belief in the principal truths of our religion. We say: "In the name" — not "names" — and thereby express our faith in the unity of God. We then mention the three Persons, the Father, the Son, and the Holy Spirit, and thereby express our belief in the Blessed Trinity.

At the same time we make the sign of the cross with our hand, thereby indicating our belief in the incarnation, death, and resurrection of the Lord. We also show that we regard him as both God and Man — for in order for him to die on the cross he had to possess a human nature.

Finally, the sign of the cross is itself a prayer made to God in the name of our Mediator Jesus Christ, who said: "Whatever you ask the Father in my name he will give you" (John 16:23).

Hence, we should make frequent use of this holy symbol of our salvation. It teaches us our true dignity. It reminds us that we are the brothers and sisters of Jesus Christ. In making the sign of the cross we become partakers in the wonderful history of our faith and companions of the glorious saints of our Church.

Another such action is the *Way of the Cross.* In this pious exercise we meditate on the sufferings that the Redeemer endured while going from the praetorium of Pilate, where he was condemned to death, to the Mount of Calvary, where he died on the cross for our salvation. We do so to put the meaning of Christ's death and resurrection into our lives.

As we meditate on the fourteen stations of the cross into which Christ's passion and death have been divided, we come to realize that the passion and death are "revelations" of the love of God the Father for all people and of Christ's love for the Father and all people. We should then be led to do in our lives what Jesus did — to give our lives in the service of others.

Sacramental Words

Sacramental words, so to speak, are words that have been made holy by the Church. They are prayers that have been time-tested, prayed by our forerunners in the faith and endorsed by the Church. They are *indulgenced prayers.*

An indulgence is the remission before God of the temporal punishment due for sins already forgiven as far as their guilt is concerned. From the spiritual treasury at her disposal made up of Christ's merits (as well as those of the Blessed Mother and the saints) the Church makes available to her members both partial and plenary indulgences.

We gain the indulgences by performing some work or saying a prayer stipulated by the Church. A partial indulgence removes part of the temporal punishment due for sin. A plenary indulgence removes all of the temporal punishment due for sin.

To acquire a plenary indulgence it is necessary to perform the work to which the indulgence is attached and to fulfill the following three conditions: (1) sacramental confession, (2) Eucharistic Communion, and (3) prayer for the intentions of the Holy Father. It is also required that all attachment to sin, even venial sin, be absent.

Ultimately, all indulgenced prayers (and works) are intended to bring us into a closer union with Christ and the Church through charity. Hence, this should also be the reason for us to do the work or say the prayer graced with indulgences.

Indulgenced prayers have an added value besides the fact of indulgences themselves. They provide us with the mind of the Church. They reproduce sentiments that the Church wants us to cultivate and possess. We need never worry that we are praying for the wrong thing.

A unique type of indulgenced prayer is found in *pious invocations*. By these we raise our hearts and minds with humble confidence to God while performing our duties or bearing the trials of life. They perfect our inward elevation. Then both the words and the inward elevation act like a precious jewel that joins our ordinary actions and adorns them.

Thus, pious invocations can be regarded as our private line to God. We can get in touch with him at any time and in every circumstance. We simply need raise our hearts and utter or only think about the pious invocation given us by the

Church. This is especially important in times of temptation or danger when it is difficult for us to say longer prayers.

An example of liturgical invocations are those uttered by many people privately at the Consecration: "My Lord and my God" at the elevation of the host and "My Jesus, mercy" at the elevation of the chalice.

Sacramental Objects

The Church has over the years placed many blessed objects at the disposal of her members. The word "object" here can refer to *person* as well as *place* or *thing*. For example, the Church now has a blessing for readers at Mass or extraordinary ministers of the Eucharist. Some of the most common sacred objects that we make use of as sacramentals are the following.

Ashes are a mark of repentance. The Church impresses them on our foreheads on Ash Wednesday, forty days before Easter, to remind us that we must prepare ourselves for receiving Christ's salvation. The minister of the ashes prays that we may keep the Lenten season in preparation for the joy of Easter. Ashes also remind us of our first beginning and our last end — and point us toward God.

Candles are used at liturgical services. They give light, which is pure, penetrates darkness, moves with incredible speed, nourishes life, and illumines all who come under its influence. Therefore, blessed candles remind us of God, the all-pure, the all-powerful, vivifier of all things, and the source of all grace and enlightenment. They also bring to our mind Christ and his salvation. He is the Light of the World who came to enlighten all those who sit in darkness and the shadow of death.

Crucifixes are representations of our Savior nailed to the cross. As such they are one of the most important sacramentals of our religion. Blessed crucifixes have the power to move us to acts of love for Christ and sincere sorrow for sin.

Images (medals and statues) of Christ, Mary, and the saints help us give honor to those they represent. They help us show adoration to our Lord, and they help us show veneration for Mary and the saints. Such images move us to pray to our heavenly Mother to intercede for us with her Son. They also prompt us to pray to the saints to offer their prayers to God on our behalf because they are with him and have great love for us.

Incense is an aromatic gum in the form of powder or grains that gives off a fragrant smoke when burned. It is used during liturgical services. By its burning, incense reminds us that we should have zeal for the things of God. By its fragrance, it reminds us to seek the "odor of sanctity." By its *rising* smoke, it tells us that our prayers have the power to rise to God.

Palms are emblems of spiritual victory just as olive branches are emblems of peace. They recall Christ's triumphal entry into Jerusalem before his death. They thus remind us of our ultimate victory in Christ if we remain faithful to him. By means of the palms we also acclaim Jesus our Messiah and King, and through them we hope one day to reach the happiness of the new and everlasting Jerusalem by faithfully following him.

Rosaries are blessed objects used in devotional prayer in honor of Mary and her Son. Through the use of the rosary we are able to meditate on the joyous, sorrowful, and glorious mysteries in the life of Jesus as well as his Mother. The rosary has been called "the compendium of the entire Gospel" (Pius XII). Meditation on the mysteries familiarizes us with the mysteries of Christ. It can thus be an excellent preparation for the celebration of those same mysteries in the liturgical action as well as a continuing echo of them.

Scapulars are two small pieces of cloth joined by strings

and worn around the neck and under the clothing. They are usually scapulars of Mary. The Brown Scapular is the best known. The scapulars remind us of Mary. They prompt us to pray to her to intercede on our behalf with Jesus. They also carry with us the prayers the Church offers for those who make use of the scapulars in their lives.

Vestments are the garments worn by the ministers of God in the performance of their duties. Vestments are set apart by the Church to excite good thoughts and to increase devotion in those who see and those who use them.

Sacramental Places

From the beginning the Church has set aside sacred places for worship. This indicates that God is there in a presence that differs from his usual presence in all creation. God is there with a more grace-laden presence.

All churches are sacred places. When we participate in liturgical actions in them, we are assured that God's grace is available in abundance for us and for the whole world. In the words of the patriarch Jacob concerning a sacred place in his day: "How awesome is this shrine! This is nothing else but an abode of God and that is the gateway to heaven" (Genesis 28:17).

It is one of the functions of the church building to fashion us into spiritual stones that make up the building that is Christ: "The liturgy daily builds up those who are within [the church] into a dwelling place for God in the Spirit, to the mature measure of the fullness of Christ" (Vatican II: *Constitution on the Sacred Liturgy*, no. 2).

In addition to churches there are sacred shrines where God grants special favors on those who come to pray there. Some of the most famous are: the holy places in Palestine; the holy house of Loreto, Italy; Our Lady of Lourdes in France; Our Lady of Fatima in Portugal; Our Lady of Guadalupe in Mexico; St. Anne de Beaupre in Canada; and Our Lady of Czestochowa in Poland.

The Church also uses ordinary buildings and blesses them so that they become sacramentals, as we have seen: libraries, workplaces, houses, and the like.

Sacramental Times

The Church, which lives in time and has her mission in time, has taken the days, the months, and the year and imbued them with the reality of the Redemption. Time itself glorifies God.

She has done this through the Liturgical Year, which we have already touched upon. At this point, we want to treat of this Liturgical Year as a sacramental. It is intended as an aid to make our faith stronger and to prepare us to serve God more generously.

We are used to many kinds of divisions of the year — the civil year (January 1 to December 31), the scholastic year (September to June), the agricultural year (seeding time to harvest time), the commercial year (January to June and June to January), and the like. It should come as no surprise then that there is also a Liturgical Year.

It is a year that was fashioned by the Church over the centuries and under the influence of the Holy Spirit given her by Christ to enable her to proclaim the Good News throughout the ages to all peoples. Broadly speaking, this year is an orderly succession of sacred times and feasts established by the Church.

Its primary function is to prolong the worship of and true dialogue with the Heavenly Father that Jesus achieved by his life, death, and resurrection. Hence, it enables us to encounter this saving Paschal Mystery of Jesus in signs and to render fitting worship to the Father in Christ and through the Holy Spirit. At the same time, it empowers us to attain the saving benefits that Jesus obtained once and for all.

During the sacred seasons of the *Liturgical Year*, the Church forms us in the faith by means of pious practices, instruction, prayer, and works of penance and mercy. But the most important role in this liturgical formation is played by each one of us.

Through the sentiments to be inculcated in us through each season we are to relive the mysteries of Christ each year. In this way we gain grace and understanding. Indeed, Pope Pius XII insisted that the Liturgical Year "is Christ himself in his Church":

> The Liturgical Year, devotedly fostered and accompanied by the Church, is not a cold and lifeless representation of the events of the past, or a simple and bare record of a former age. It is rather Christ himself who is ever living in his Church. Here he continues that journey of immense mercy that he lovingly began in his mortal life, going about doing good with the design of bringing human beings to know his mysteries and in a way live by them.
>
> These mysteries are ever present and active not in a vague and uncertain way as some modern writers hold, but in the way that Catholic doctrine teaches us. According to the Doctors of the Church, [these mysteries] are shining examples of Christian perfection, as well as sources of divine grace, owing to the merit and prayers of Christ; they still influence us because each mystery brings its own special grace for us (*Encyclical on the Sacred Liturgy*, no. 165).

The Church continually asks for us in her prayers those gifts that would give us the greatest possible share in the spirit of these mysteries through the merits of Christ. By living the *Liturgical Year* fully, we can transform ourselves into true followers of Christ.

9

PRAYING
WITH THE SACRAMENTALS

The People of God have always been associated with a large variety of signs found in the history of salvation. This is true of the Old Testament, the New Testament, and the time of the Church in which we are situated.

Creation harbors a kind of first order of sacred sign. The Fathers of the Church found "vestiges" and images of God therein. Light, for example, is a sign of God's glorious splendor and unsurpassed love. The stability of the universe and the earth is a sign of God's truth and fidelity. Human beings constitute a sign of God's goodness and concern by their power to know good and evil and their love for each other.

Jesus himself made use of natural signs to communicate his message of salvation as well as the salvation itself. He used water, a sign of death and life, to make us die to the life of sin and be born to the life of the Spirit. He used a meal, a sign of fraternal communion, to institute a sacrament of unity in his love.

There are in human experience a great variety of vestiges of God if only they are perceived. Almost everything in a person's life can be made to reflect the Divinity in some way or other. Almost everything in the world can be used to impart the message of Revelation provided it is used in the right way.

> All the events of our Christian life — in the measure in which they are read in the light of faith in the dead and risen Christ; all our visible activities whether spiritual or temporal — in the measure in which they are filled with love for Christ offering himself — also constitute for us in their way expressive signs of the language of the God who saves and sanctifies the world (Joseph Gelineau, "The Nature and Role of Signs in the Economy of the Covenant" in *Worship* 39 [November 1965], p. 530).

Thus, the liturgy is itself replete with a language of symbolism. Some of it comes from the Biblical symbolism and some from the ordinary life of the people of the times in which the liturgical rites were put together.

This means that the language of the liturgy is an elaborated language. It is much more historical than natural, much more personal than physical, and much more social than individual.

Through this liturgical language and its rite, God is worshiped and we receive sanctification as well as enlightenment concerning the true relationship between God and us. And this is all effected through Jesus Christ, the Christian Symbol beyond compare and God's definitive Word to humankind.

By praying *with* the Sacramentals, we will more readily enter into the meaning of these signs. This type of praying will teach us as it prepares us for receiving the sacraments.

Praying with the sacramentals also provides us with beautiful prayers for practically every occasion in our lives.

Praying with Sacramental Blessings

The blessings, as we have already indicated, present us with a wide variety of prayers that we can use in our everyday lives. As we use these prayers, we should be conscious that they enable us to Christify our world.

Whether we are working or at leisure, serving the public or watching a baseball game on television, we can bring that event into tune with the history of salvation. We can make each event grace-laden through our prayer.

If we work in an *office* a quiet prayer of blessing will serve to help Christify it:

> O God,
> in your wise providence
> you are glad to bless all human labor,
> the work of our hands and of our mind.
> Grant that all who plan and conduct business in this office
> may through your guidance and support
> come to right decisions and carry them out fairly.
> We ask this through Christ our Lord.

If you work in a factory, an equally quiet recitation of the following prayer will do wonders for it:

> O God,
> by working as a carpenter
> your Son enhanced the dignity of human labor
> and in a wonderful way joined us
> through our own toil to the work of redemption.
> Through the blessing they seek,
> strengthen your faithful.
> Give to those who are employed in skillfully transforming
> the things you have created

sense of their own dignity.
Make them content in their dedication
to bettering the human family
in praise of your name.
We ask this through Christ our Lord.

If you work in a shop, there is also a prayer that fits right
in with your circumstances:

God, our all-provident Father,
you have placed the earth and its fruits under our care,
so that by our labor we will endeavor
to insure that all share in the benefits of your creation.
Bless all those who will use this building
either as buyers or as sellers,
so that by respecting justice and charity
they will see themselves as working for the common good
and find joy in contributing to the progress of
    the earthly city.
We ask this through Christ our Lord.

If you are ready to enjoy a television sporting event, you
can recite a short prayer that will bring it too into the circle of
salvation history:

Strong and faithful God,
as we come together for this contest,
we ask you to bless these athletes.
Keep them safe from injury and harm,
instill in them respect for each other,
and reward them for their perseverance.
Lead us all to the rewards of your kingdom
where you live and reign for ever and ever.

If you seek a prayer for your family, you can use the
following, which is a prayer of Christian life:

O God,
you have created us in love and saved us in mercy,
and through the bond of marriage
you have established the family
and willed that it should become a sign of Christ's love
    for his Church.
Shower your blessings on this family gathered here in
    your name.
Enable those who are joined by one love
to support one another
by their fervor of spirit and devotion to prayer.
Make them responsive to the needs of others
and witnesses to the faith in all they say and do.
We ask this through Christ our Lord.

If you have children, there is a prayer for them that can bring special joy to your heart:

Father,
inexhaustible source of life and author of all good,
we bless and we thank you
for brightening our communion of love by your gift
    of children.
Grant that our children will find in the life of this family
    such inspiration
that they will strive always for what is right and good
and one day, by your grace,
reach their home in heaven.
We ask this through Christ our Lord.

If you desire a prayer for older members of the family or older friends, the Church has a perfect one:

Lord, our God,
you have given these your faithful
the grace to maintain their hope in you

through all life's changes
and to taste and see your goodness.
We bless you for the gifts you have showered on them
    for so many years.
We ask that they may find joy in a renewed strength of spirit,
that they may have good health,
and that they may inspire us by the example of their serene
    way of life.
We ask this through Christ our Lord.

There is also a prayer of thanksgiving for any occasion by
which we can thank God for all he has done for us:

Almighty Father,
you are lavish in bestowing all your gifts,
and we give you thanks for the favors you have given to us.
In your goodness you have favored us
and kept us safe in the past.
We ask that you continue to protect us
and to shelter us in the shadow of your wings.
We ask this through Christ our Lord.

Praying with Indulgenced Prayers

There is something very comforting about praying with
indulgenced prayers. We know that they are the prayers the
Church wants us to use. They reproduce sentiments that the
Church wants us to cultivate and possess. Thus, they can be of
immense benefit to our spiritual lives.

One of the finest indulgenced prayers is the prayer before
a crucifix to be said after Communion:

Look down upon me,
good and gentle Jesus,
while before your face I humbly kneel,

and with burning soul pray and beseech you
to fix deep in my heart
lively sentiments of faith, hope and charity,
true contrition for my sins,
and a firm purpose of amendment,
while I contemplate with great love and tender pity
your five wounds,
pondering over them within me
calling to mind the words which David, your prophet,
said of you, my good Jesus:
"They have pierced my hands and my feet;
they have numbered all my bones."

Another favorite prayer of many people is the prayer to
Christ the King:

Most sweet Jesus,
Redeemer of the human race,
look down upon us humbly prostrate before you.
We are yours, and yours we wish to be;
but to be more surely united with you,
behold, each one of us freely consecrates
    himself/herself today
to your Most Sacred Heart.
Many indeed have never known you;
many, too, despising your precepts,
have rejected you.
Have mercy on them all, most merciful Jesus,
and draw them to your Sacred Heart.

Be King, O Lord,
not only of the faithful who have never forsaken you
but also of the prodigal children who have
    abandoned you;
grant that they may quickly return to their Father's house,
lest they die of wretchedness and hunger.

Be King of those who are deceived by erroneous opinions,
or whom discord keeps aloof,
and call them back to the harbor of truth
and the unity of faith,
so that soon there may be but one flock and one Shepherd.

Grant, O Lord, to your Church
assurance of freedom and immunity from harm;
give tranquility of order to all nations;
make the earth resound from pole to pole with one cry:
Praise to the divine Heart that wrought our salvation;
to it be glory and honor for ever.

We also have at hand indulgenced prayers to Mary, the
Mother of God, that she may intercede for us. The beautiful
Hail Holy Queen is one such prayer:

Hail, holy Queen, Mother of mercy;
hail, our life, our sweetness, and our hope.
To you do we cry
poor banished children of Eve.
To you do we send up our sighs,
mourning and weeping in this valley of tears.
Turn then, most gracious Advocate,
your eyes of mercy toward us.
And after this our exile
show unto us the blessed fruit of your womb, Jesus.
O clement, O loving, O sweet Virgin Mary.

As we have mentioned, we also have available *indulgenced invocations*. These are like telegrams that we can
send off to God, to Jesus, to Mary and the saints. Some of the
more popular ones are:

May Jesus Christ be praised.

* * *

Thanks be to God.

Your will be done.

*   *   *

Most Sacred Heart of Jesus, I place my trust in you.

*   *   *

My God and my all.

*   *   *

My Lord and My God.

*   *   *

Jesus, meek and humble of heart,
make my heart like your Heart.

*   *   *

My Jesus, mercy.

*   *   *

Sweet heart of Mary, be my salvation.

*   *   *

Queen, conceived without original sin, pray for us.

There are many other invocations that are no longer indulgenced. We could say any one of these. They are found in *The Raccolta*. Some of them are:

O God, come to my assistance.
O Lord, make haste to help me.

*   *   *

Jesus, Son of the living God, have mercy on us.

*   *   *

Jesus, my God, I love you above all things.

*   *   *

God the Holy Spirit, have mercy on us.

*   *   *

Virgin most sorrowful, pray for us.

Praying in Sacred Places

We can pray to Christ in the Blessed Sacrament in our churches. In time of difficulty, we can even pray at home as if we were visiting him there. The following is one of the many prayers that the Church has endorsed in the past:

> I adore you, O Jesus,
> true God and true man,
> here present in the Holy Eucharist.
> As I humbly kneel before you,
> I unite myself in spirit with
> all the faithful on earth
> and all the blessed in heaven.
> In deep gratitude for so great a blessing,
> I offer you my wholehearted love, dear Lord,
> for you are all perfect
> and all worthy of love.
> Grant me the grace to never offend you again
> and to be refreshed by your Eucharistic presence
> here on earth,
> so that with Mary
> I may enjoy your eternal and ever blessed presence
> in heaven.

We can also pray to Mary in her shrines — by being there in person or by being there in our mind's eye. The following prayer is that of Pope John Paul II to Our Lady of Guadalupe, the Patroness of our hemisphere:

> O Immaculate Virgin,
> Mother of the true God and Mother of the Church,
> from this spot you have manifested
> your clemency and your compassion
> for all who have recourse to your protection.
> Hear the prayer we direct to you with filial confidence

and present it to your Son Jesus,
our only Redeemer.

Mother of mercy,
Teacher of hidden and silent sacrifice,
we sinners consecrate to you,
who come to meet us,
all our being and all our love.
We also consecrate to you
our life, our work, our joys, our infirmities, and our sorrows.

Grant to our peoples peace, justice, and prosperity
so that we may entrust to your care,
our Lady and our Mother,
all that we have and all that we are.

We wish to be completely yours
and to follow together with you
the path of total fidelity to Jesus Christ
in his Church;
hold us ever lovingly by the hand.

Praying in Accord with the Liturgical Seasons

As we have seen, the Church has evolved a plan for us to live Christ's mysteries throughout the year. If we live in tune with the seasons of the Liturgical Year, we will grow spiritually. There are many ways in which this can be done.

We can use the prayers of the liturgy for the season. We can meditate on the Scripture readings used during the season. Or we can compose prayers according to the theme of the season.

An excellent and easy way of doing so is by using the Church's prayers before and after meals — with their seasonal antiphons:

Before Meals

The eyes of all creatures look to you
to give them food in due time.

R. You give it to them, they gather it up;
You open your hand, they have their fill.

Let us call on the name of the Father,
who always takes care of his children.

R. Our Father . . . but deliver us from evil.
    For the kingdom, the power, and the glory are yours,
    now and for ever. Amen.

Bless us, O Lord, and these your gifts
which we are about to receive from your goodness.
Through Christ our Lord.

R. Amen.

After Meals

Let all your works praise you, O Lord.
R. Let all your peoples bless you.

We give you thanks for all your gifts, almighty God,
living and reigning now and for ever.

R. Amen.

For the sake of your name, O Lord,
reward those who have been good to us
and give them eternal life.

R. Amen.

Or:

Lord, give all people the food they need,
so that they may join us in giving you thanks.

R. Amen.

The following verses are substituted according to the seasons of the year:

Before Meals during Advent

Give ear, O Lord and shepherd of your people.
R. Stir up your power and come.

After Meals during Advent

Let us live soberly, justly, and devoutly in this world.
R. As we wait in joyful hope for the coming of our Savior, Jesus Christ.

Before Meals during the Christmas Season

The Word became flesh, alleluia.
R. And dwelt among us, alleluia.

After Meals during the Christmas Season

The Lord has made known, alleluia.
R. His saving power, alleluia.

Before Meals during Lent

No one lives on bread alone.
R. But on every word that comes from the mouth of God.

After Meals during Lent

A time of penance has been granted us.
R. To atone for our sins and heal our souls.

Before and After Meals during Easter Triduum

For our sake Christ was obedient, accepting even death.
R. Death on a cross.

Before and After Meals during Easter Week

This is the day the Lord has made, alleluia.
R. Let us rejoice and be glad, alleluia.

Before Meals during the Easter Season
With glad and generous hearts all who believed
took their meals in common, alleluia.
R. Praising God, alleluia.

After Meals during the Easter Season
R. In the breaking of the bread, alleluia.

We can also pray by according a mystery of Christ to each month of the year. These are not as hard and fast as are the themes of the liturgical seasons, but they enable us to meditate on the pertinent aspect of our faith as we pray day by day. The following is an approved pattern for monthly themes together with a sample prayer:

January — The Holy Name of Jesus
February — The Sacred Passion
March — St. Joseph
April — The Holy Eucharist
May — The Blessed Virgin Mary
June — The Sacred Heart of Jesus
July — The Precious Blood of Jesus
August — The Immaculate Heart of Mary
September — Our Lady Queen of Martyrs
October — The Most Holy Rosary
November — The Faithful Departed
December — The Holy Infancy

Prayer for February

O God,
for the redemption of the world
you will to be born among human beings
to be circumcised,
to be rejected by your people,

to be betrayed by Judas with a kiss,
to be bound with cords,
to be led to slaughter as an innocent lamb,
and to be shamelessly exposed to the gaze of Annas,
    Caiaphas, Pilate, and Herod.

You willed to be accused by false witnesses,
to be tormented by scourges and insults,
to be defiled with spitting,
to be crowned with thorns,
to be smitten with blows,
to be struck with a reed,
to be blindfolded and stripped of your garments,
to be fastened to the cross and lifted up on it,
to be reckoned among the wicked,
to be given gall and vinegar to drink,
and to be pierced with a lance.

O Lord,
by these holy sufferings,
upon which I meditate to the best of my ability,
and by your holy cross and death,
deliver me from the pains of hell
and bring me to that paradise
where you brought the penitent thief crucified with you
and where you live and reign
with the Father and the Holy Spirit for ever.

Another pattern of prayer in the Church assigns a theme
to every day of the week. The following is an approved pattern
for daily themes together with a sample prayer.

Sunday — The Blessed Trinity
Monday — The Holy Spirit
Tuesday — The Angels and Saints
Wednesday — St. Joseph

Thursday — The Blessed Sacrament
Friday — The Holy Cross
Saturday — The Blessed Virgin Mary

Prayer for Sunday

Most holy Trinity,
Father, Son, and Holy Spirit,
behold us prostrate in your divine presence.
We humble ourselves profoundly
and beg of you the pardon of our sins.

We adore you,
almighty Father,
and with overflowing hearts we thank you
for having given us your divine Son Jesus
as our Redeemer.
He gave himself to us in the most august Eucharist
even to the ends of the earth,
revealing unto us the wondrous love of his heart
in this mystery of faith and love.

We adore you,
Word of God,
dear Jesus our Redeemer,
and with overflowing hearts we thank you
for having taken human flesh
and having become priest and victim
for our redemption
in the sacrifice of the cross —
a sacrifice that,
through the exceeding love of your Sacred Heart,
you renew upon our altars at every moment.
O high priest and divine victim,
give us the grace to honor your holy sacrifice
in the most adorable Eucharist

with the homage of Mary most holy
and of all your Church.
We offer ourselves wholly to you,
In your infinite goodness, accept our offering,
unite it to your own,
and grant us your blessing.

We adore you,
Divine Spirit,
and with overflowing hearts we thank you
for having wrought the ineffable blessing
of the Incarnation of the Word of God,
a blessing that is being continually extended
and increased in the holy sacrament of the Eucharist.
By this adorable mystery of the love
of the Sacred Heart of Jesus,
grant us and all poor sinners your holy grace.
Pour forth your holy gifts upon us
and upon all redeemed souls,
especially the Pope,
all cardinals, bishops, and pastors,
as well as priests and other ministers of your sanctuary.

10

PRAYING
THE LITURGY OF THE HOURS

In addition to the prayer of the Eucharist and the sacraments, there is a second public prayer of Christ and his Church — or to be more precise another aspect of that prayer — the Liturgy of the Hours. This was once called the *Breviary*, and it is a way in which the entire day can be made holy by the praises of God.

This prayer too — which technically is classified as a sacramental — is part of Christ's priesthood. In the Holy Spirit, Christ carries out through the Church the work of humankind's glorification — as he also does in the Eucharist and in other ways. In the Liturgy of the Hours, Christ himself is priest, in the assembled community, in the proclamation of God's Word, and in the prayer and song of the Church.

The experience of time (principally communicated through hours) in our modern way of life is undergoing a profound evolution. People who lived before modern times were used to slow rhythms. We live in an electronic and computerized age, one characterized by ever-increasing speed that impinges on nerves and spirit.

The rhythms of our lives are no longer those of nature — day, night, months, weeks, seasons — but those of industrialized labor. The basic unit is no longer the day but the week. And a new rhythm is emerging — the alternation of work and leisure time. The week is made up of five days of labor and two of rest. The time of rest is no longer Sunday but the end of each week — the weekend.

To this weekly rhythm are added others: months of work and months of vacation; times of movement from place of work to place of residence. And above it all is the all-pervading influence of the means of social communication. The newspaper substitutes for our morning prayer and the television replaces our evening prayer.

In such a situation there is need to sanctify time. We must sanctify not only the day, not some mathematical and imperial time, not some abstract and empty space, but a concrete, living, personal time. This is the time of history given rhythm by days, nights, and seasons as well as by our organic life in its active and resting phases. It is the time of our whole being.

The Liturgy of the Hours places in our hands a tremendous instrument for prolonging the worship of Christ throughout the day, the dialogue of love flowing between the Father and the Son for all eternity, which is memorialized in the Eucharist. When we pray the Hours, ours is no longer a prayer of an individual person; grace and the universal priesthood bestowed on us at baptism make our prayer the prayer of Christ and his whole body.

The Liturgy of the Hours is a veritable treasury of prayer at our disposal. When used judiciously, it can help us sanctify all the circumstances of our busy daily life and all the attitudes of our changing inner life.

A Liturgy "of the Hours"

This liturgy that complements the Eucharist has various names (Work of God, Divine Office, and Sacrifice of Praise among others), but its most suitable name is "Liturgy of the Hours." It deals with "hours," that is, temporal articulations of the day. Each part of this liturgy has for its purpose to sanctify a particular moment or part of the day. And this is not some secondary or peripheral aspect. It is an essential one that is important for our spiritual lives.

The Liturgy of the Hours accompanies the day with a rhythm of prayer by choosing characteristic moments of daily life. It gives the Divine an opportunity to make its way into the very texture of our days.

The Divine Office focuses on the light of day and makes it the visible sign of the two aspects of the memorial of Christ. Christ is first the light of the divine knowledge infused into us, the Author and Finisher of our faith (Hebrews 12:2). He is also the light in which the glory of God communicated to us through his resurrection shines forth.

Thus, the hour marked by prayer is transported out of the empty flow of cosmic time into the sphere of the divine, and those who experience such an hour acquire roots in eternity. At the same time, the hour in question applies its specific significance and natural charm to the prayer.

Dawn creates, as it were, the world anew after a night of darkness and inactivity. We too are filled with new spiritual energy. We pray that the light may shine in our hearts, as we experience a resurrection and a renewed confidence.

Midday has the connotation of heat and light (the "noonday sun"), inevitably recalling God, the Light beyond all shadows. We see this light as the symbol of the Spirit and truth and grace, which throw a spiritual radiance about the universe.

Evening brings darkness and rest from labor. It reminds us that God knows no rest from his work ("My Father is at work until now" — John 5:17). Even in darkness, he comes to watch lovingly over us ("You are my help, and in the shadow of your wings I shout for joy" — Psalm 63:8).

This night is lit up like the day, because Christ the "eternal Day" is ever with us. The alternation of light and darkness reminds us of the inconstancy of all that is human. But it also helps ground us on God.

By utilizing the Liturgy of the Hours, we can begin anew to appreciate the "traces" of God in natural creation. Indeed, we will enable creation to sing God's praises with us in company with the angels and the saints — for we are to offer praise "in the name of every creature under heaven" (Eucharistic Prayer IV).

The Liturgy of the Hours also provides us with a convenient way for reliving all the stages of Christ's mystery. The hours are laid down according to the sun's course, and the sun is a symbol of Christ. The sun's rising is the most striking image of the Savior rising from the dead — and in fact the hour of his rising.

Midday is the time he was nailed to the cross and the hour of his ascension as well, the high noon of his life. *Midafternoon* corresponds with the hour at which he died on the cross. And *midmorning* recalls the outpouring of the Holy Spirit.

Accordingly, every moment of our lives becomes a "time of salvation" for us through the Liturgy of the Hours — if we but take hold of it and use it.

Action and Prayer

Jesus has left us the example of a life balanced perfectly on action and prayer. "Each day's work was closely connected and in fact flowed out of that prayer. . . . The Divine Master showed that prayer was the soul of his Messianic ministry and Paschal Death" (*General Introduction of the Liturgy of the Hours*, no. 4).

The Liturgy of the Hours is to be prayed in this spirit by us. Each hour should be a key moment that embraces the ongoing reality comprising the whole of life. It should be a radiant moment in which a lived reality that sustains our being finds expression in a visible communal form.

If carried out in this spirit, the Liturgy of the Hours will enable us to see Christ in all things — in every event and action of our lives. These are signs that hold him, and when we pierce them we encounter him. We are "strengthened to bring the Good News of Christ to those outside" (*Ibid.*, no. 18). Each hour becomes a new impetus to apostolic activity.

The Liturgy of the Hours fosters our encounter with Christ and links our lives with his. By its relation with various hours of our day, it accomplishes this purpose through a kind of "osmotic action" that pervades the day with prayer.

Through the saving power of the Eucharist, of which it is an extension, the Office makes us ever more perfectly love Christ — if only we let it. It makes us "living sacraments" of him. In the words of St. Ambrose:

> May the image [of Christ] shine forth in our profession of faith, in our love, and in our words and actions, so that his whole likeness may be mirrored in us, if possible. May he be our head because "Christ is our Head." May he be our eye so that through him we may see the Father. May he be our voice with which we speak to the Father. And may he be the hand with which we offer the sacrifice of our lives to God the Father (*Concerning Isaac and the Soul*, 8, 75).

The Liturgy of the Hours is a continuation of the prayer of Christ. A lively participation in it will impart to us a desire to live out our identification with Christ in prayer. It will help us feel that his prayer is being uttered through our mouth just as his life resides in the life of grace in us. It will also lead to a deeper spiritual life.

At the same time, the Liturgy of the Hours is a prayer of the Church, which is the Body of Christ. We pray this prayer as a community — never in isolation. When we pray it, we are in tune with the Church. It enables us to become interpreters of all the Church's needs.

In our tears, the Church weeps for all who mourn. In our joys, she rejoices with all who are glad. In our repentance, she does penance for all who repent. The main concerns of the kingdom of God become our concerns.

The Liturgy of the Hours is made up of many elements. Reflection on the most outstanding ones will help us to participate better in this wonderful prayer.

The Psalms

The major role is played by the Psalms. This alone would give the Liturgy of the Hours a unique hue. The Psalms are the prayer of God's assembly, the public prayer of the People of God.

We have already said a word about the Psalms concerning their use as Responsorial Psalms at Mass. Here we might profitably dwell on other particulars about them.

We must remember that the Psalms are poetry. They must always be read as poetry in order to be understood. The poetry of the Psalms makes use of assonance, rhyme, refrains, word plays, and acrostics. It is devoid of self-consciousness and free of artificial language.

The Psalms contain rhythm, which is the recurrence of accented or unaccented syllables at regular intervals. But their outstanding trait is the parallelism symptomatic of all Hebrew poetry — the equal distribution or balance of thought in the various lines of each verse.

Synonymous parallelism is the repetition of the same thought with equivalent expressions:

> He who sits in the heavens laughs;
> the Lord is laughing them to scorn (Psalm 2:4)

Antithetic parallelism expresses a thought by contrast with an opposite:

> For the Lord guards the way of the just
> but the way of the wicked leads to doom (Psalm 1:6).

Synthetic parallelism occurs when a second line completes the thoughts of the first by giving a comparison:

> I cry out to the Lord.
> He answers from his holy mountain.
> I lie down to rest and I sleep.
> I wake, for the Lord upholds me (Psalm 3:5-6).

If we remain conscious of this beautiful feature of the poetry of the Psalms, we will be able to pray them all the more devoutly. We will pray them meaningfully and intelligently.

As far as content, the Psalms also have a few outstanding qualities. They are very objective in their praise of God. They reproduce praise that is simple, dignified, and direct. They enable us to praise God as he ought to be praised.

These sacred poems are also filled with implicit faith. They express human need and affliction in passionate and almost rebellious tones. But they stress that God is ready to hear and deliver. These are precisely the characteristics that we seek in our prayers.

The Psalms convey an awareness of the moral obligations that are inspired in worship. They thus keep us close to God's way of looking at things.

The Psalms also portray a note of joy in the thanksgivings — a joy that was one of the key elements of Israelite worship and that should be a key element in our worship as well. We can relate it to the salvation that Christ extends to each of us — which should be for us the greatest of all joys.

However, one of the most attractive characteristics of the Psalms is that they are the prayers of Jesus. As a devout member of the chosen people, Jesus must have prayed the Psalms hundreds of times. When we pray them, we are more closely joined to Christ in this praying. We can say that we are praying in the very words of Jesus (through the magic of translation, of course).

The Readings

The Readings from Scripture that are found in the Liturgy of the Hours have a different function from the Readings at Mass. They are not so much proclamations to move us to worship as meditations on the Word of God. They are meant to be listened to in a spirit of openness and to shape our thinking as the Spirit wills.

In a sense, these Readings have the character of a retreat or a day of recollection with the Holy Spirit as our guide. God still speaks to us today. The Readings have a message that is special to us.

God's Word is now filled with the Spirit, whose influence is exercised no longer through the sacred writer but through the Word that is placed in my hand or sounded in my ears. However, this is only true if we read the Readings "in tune with the Church." She is the living organism that transmits the Word to us and is alone able to grasp its full meaning.

We cannot approach this Word as mere "spectators." We are not encountering just a "piece of paper" or a "dead letter." We are attaining a personal encounter with the living God who addresses us and wants us to respond to him.

The Readings are thus dialogal, meditational, and prayerful. At the same time, they are Readings that impart wisdom — one that goes beyond mere scientific knowledge and wisdom. Finally, they are Readings that lead to action.

The Readings also include texts from the Fathers of the Church, which comment on the Bible texts or elaborate some theme or idea found therein. In this way the Church acquaints us with our great forerunners in the faith and makes us the beneficiaries of their thoughts.

Another type of reading is also included — the hagiographical reading. This is an extract from a writing of the saint of the day or a text from a short biography of the saint or a text that brings out some aspect of his or her personality.

In this way, the Church stresses that the saints are "sacred pages" through which God addresses the world. They are "Gospels" endowed with a new realism because they are filled inwardly with the Spirit of Christ. The saints are living interpretations of Scripture, bits of authentically existential exegesis. By following them, we will not go wrong.

The Responsories

The Church helps us to obtain the right interpretation of the Readings found in the Liturgy of the Hours. She does this through the Responsories that come immediately after them.

The Responsories: (1) shed light on the Readings that precede them; (2) they situate the Readings in the History of Salvation; (3) they project on the Readings the content of the Old and the New Testaments; (4) finally, they turn the Readings into prayer and contemplation.

Through the aid of feasts and memorials, the Church also ensures that the Word of God found in the Readings becomes more than God's revelation. The Church transforms that Word into an initiation into the Mystery that is being lived in the liturgical *today* of the Church.

If we concentrate on the means placed at our disposal in the Liturgy of the Hours, we can attain what the Church desires for each of us. We can arrive at the spiritual sense of each Reading in addition to the literal sense. And we can acquire the inner dispositions to relive it today by means of our personal response.

A similar process takes place with regard to the non-Biblical Readings. The Responsories enable us to meditate on them in such a way that the Readings become part of our spiritual treasury. They teach us how to live the Christian life in our circumstances of life — in imitation of the saints who preceded us along the way.

The Intercessions and Prayers

One of the entirely new elements of the Liturgy of the Hours is the Intercessions introduced into the Hours of Morning Prayer and Evening Prayer. This amounts to a series of some 200 prayer formulas that offer a rich and varied moment in each Hour dedicated to prayer of petition.

In order to avoid making these duplicates of the General Intercessions at Mass, the Church has given them a different structure. These are directed to a Divine Person. Indeed, whenever possible, they are addressed to Jesus.

As a result, they take on a more human tone and a more direct impact. It also makes them correspond to a basic Christian rhythm — the movement in which we go through Jesus, who is the "Way," in order to reach the Father.

These Intercessions also include a variable response and can be carried out in varied ways. This is especially important in private recitation and in communal recitation by a very knowledgeable assembly or group.

The Intercessions at Morning Prayer refer more directly to the day that is beginning. They offer praise and thanksgiving for creation, life, prayer for a day's work and the grace to live in God, and intercession for the persons one will meet that day. The Intercessions at Evening Prayer gather up the various intentions of the world and the Church and include a prayer for the dead.

The Intercessions make us realize that our daily life has its place in the petitions the Church utters before God each morning and evening. They also help us to understand that the History of Salvation is continuing and the work of our salvation is still being accomplished in the routine of everyday activity.

Finally, there are the Concluding Prayers. Most of them are taken from the Opening Prayers found in the Sunday Masses. These are excellent prayers, as we have seen. Some seventy prayers are newly composed.

These are found for the most part in Morning Prayer and Evening Prayer as well as Daytime Prayer for Ordinary Time. They serve to emphasize the specific idea of the liturgical Hour being celebrated.

11

PRAYING WITH
THE LITURGY OF THE HOURS

As we have seen, the Liturgy of the Hours is totally devoted to prayer. It features Hymns, Psalms, Readings, Responsories, Intercessions, and Concluding Prayers. One hour could be outlined as follows:

Introduction
Hymn
Psalmody

    Morning Prayer: Psalm, Old Testament Canticle, and Psalm with their Antiphons

    Evening Prayer: two Psalms, New Testament Canticle, with their Antiphons

Biblical Reading
Responsory
Gospel Canticle (of Mary or Zechariah) with its Antiphon
Intercessions
Lord's Prayer
Concluding Prayer

As such, the Liturgy of the Hours represents a feast for the person who seeks prayer formulas in tune with the Church. Cardinal Anthony Poma has nicely summarized the prayer riches that are found in it:

> [The Liturgy of the Hours] has the capacity to include and express the most profound and universal sentiments of our human life. It offers a gamut of invocations, which are intoned at the various hours of the day. It touches and interprets the different moments of activity: morning, work, fatigue, and rest. It penetrates the varying conditions and elevates the values of human life: difficulties, temptations, poverty, suffering, love of neighbor, social events, peace, fear, and personal and social needs. Above all, it represents a continual reference to the salvific deeds, the continuous assistance that comes from Christ. It makes us experience always the vital love of Mary, associated with the Redemption of her Son and the diffusion of his grace.
>
> Therein is found, together with the nourishment that comes from the Word of God, the voice that has been transmitted to us across the distant centuries, that is given us by the Church in actual conditions of her history, and also by the spirituality and testimony of the saints, who in every age have illumined the journey of the People of God ("The Church That Prays in Time" in *La Liturgia delle Ore*, Turin: Marietti, 1980, p. 24).

This means that we have at hand a wonderful instrument for prayer. We can pray with almost every element found in the Liturgy of the Hours. For it contains nothing but elements for prayer.

The complete Liturgy of the Hours is found in four volumes. However, there is a one-volume edition entitled *Christian Prayer*, which contains all that is needed by the average person. In fact, there is an even smaller edition entitled *Shorter Christian Prayer* that will also suffice.

By utilizing any one of these editions, we can have prayers galore that fit in with any part of our lives. The following selections give an idea of the treasury of prayers that lies waiting for us.

Praying with the Psalms

The Psalms offer numerous formulas of prayer for us. They cover almost every type of emotion or situation. There are Psalms of thanksgiving, lament, devotion, prayer, grief, praise, confession, repentance, and meditation.

Are you seeking comfort in time of trial or fear? Try Psalm 27, which is used in Evening Prayer of Wednesday in Week I:

Psalm 27: God Stands by Us in Dangers

The Lord is my light and my help;
whom shall I fear?
The Lord is the stronghold of my life;
before whom shall I shrink?

When evil-doers draw near
to devour my flesh,
it is they, my enemies and foes,
who stumble and fall.

Though an army encamp against me
my heart would not fear.
Though war break out against me
even then would I trust.

There is one thing I ask of the Lord,
for this I long,
to live in the house of the Lord,

all the days of my life,
to savor the sweetness of the Lord,
to behold his temple.

For there he keeps me safe in his tent
in the day of evil.
He hides me in the shelter of his tent,
on a rock he sets me safe.

And now my head shall be raised
above my foes who surround me
and I shall offer within his tent
a sacrifice of joy.

I will sing and make music for the Lord.

Are you in need of a prayer for pardon and peace? You can do no better than make use of Psalm 130, which is found in Evening Prayer I of Sunday in Week IV:

Psalm 130: A Cry from the Depths

Out of the depths I cry to you, O Lord,
Lord, hear my voice!
O let your ears be attentive
to the voice of my pleading.

If you, O Lord, should mark our guilt,
Lord, who would survive?
But with you is found forgiveness;
for this we revere you.

My soul is waiting for the Lord, I count on his word.
My soul is longing for the Lord
more than watchman for daybreak.
Let the watchman count on daybreak
and Israel on the Lord.

Because with the Lord there is mercy
and fullness of redemption,

Israel indeed he will redeem
from all its iniquity.

Are you in need of a prayer of pure praise of God — to
show your gratitude for being alive and for having the possibil-
ity of eternal life? Psalm 150 is perfect, and it is found in
Morning Prayer of Sunday in Week IV:

Psalm 150: Praise the Lord

Praise God in his holy place,
praise him in his mighty heavens.
Praise him for his powerful deeds,
praise his surpassing greatness.

O praise him with sound of trumpet,
praise him with lute and harp.
Praise him with timbrel and dance,
praise him with strings and pipes.

O praise him with resounding cymbals,
praise him with clashing of cymbals.
Let everything that lives and that breathes
give praise to the Lord.

We may also make use of the Psalm-prayers that are
found at the bottom of each Psalm in the Liturgy of the Hours.
For example, the Psalm-prayers for each of the above Psalms
are as follows:

Psalm-prayer for Psalm 27

Father,
you protect and strengthen those who hope in you;
you heard your Son and kept him safe in your tent
in the day of evil.
Grant that your servants
who seek your face in times of trouble
may see your goodness in the land of the living.

Psalm-prayer for Psalm 130

Listen with compassion to our prayers, Lord.
The forgiveness of sins is yours.
Do not look on the wrong we have done,
but grant us your merciful kindness.

Psalm-prayer for Psalm 150

Lord God,
maker of heaven and earth and of all created things,
you make your just ones holy
and you justify sinners who confess your name.
Hear us as we humbly pray to you:
give us eternal joy with your saints.

Praying with the Readings

The Readings provide us with much beautiful material for
meditative prayer. We could select one from practically every
page. The following are simply random samples.

Do you wish to think a little about our divine adoption in
Christ? The Reading (1 John 3:1-3) for Evening Prayer of
Tuesday in Week I constitutes a good beginning:

Reading — 1 John 3:1-3

See what love the Father has bestowed on us
in letting us be called children of God!
Yet that is what we are.
The reason the world does not recognize us
is that it never recognized the Son.
Dearly beloved,
we are God's children now;
what we shall later be has not yet come to light.
We know that when it comes to light

we shall be like him,
for we shall see him as he is.
Everyone who has this hope based on him
keeps himself pure, as he is pure.

Are you seeking to dwell on a short simple rule of life?
You can do no better than the Reading from Tobit for Morning
Prayer of Wednesday in Week I:

Reading — Tobit 4:15a, 16a, 18a, 19

Do to no one what you yourself dislike.
Give to the hungry some of your bread,
and to the naked some of your clothing.
Seek counsel from every wise man.
At all times bless the Lord God,
and ask him to make all your paths straight
and to grant success to all your endeavors and plans.

Are you in need of courage in the face of adversity? Turn
to the Reading from Paul's Letter to the Romans found in
Morning Prayer of Wednesday in Week II:

Reading — Romans 8:35-39

Who will separate us from the love of Christ?
Trial, or distress, or persecution, or hunger,
    or nakedness, or danger, or the sword?
As Scripture says:
"For your sake we are being slain all the day long;
we are looked upon as sheep to be slaughtered."
Yet in all this we are more than conquerors
because of him who has loved us.
For I am certain that neither death nor life,
neither angels nor principalities,
neither the present nor the future,
nor powers,

neither height nor depth,
nor any other creature,
will be able to separate us
from the love of God
that comes to us in Christ Jesus, our Lord.

Perhaps you want to meditate on the gratuitousness of
God's salvation that is offered to us in Christ. You can ponder
the words of the great prophet Isaiah found in Morning Prayer
of Tuesday in Week IV:

Reading — Isaiah 55:1-3

All you who are thirsty,
    come to the water!
You who have no money,
    come, receive grain and eat;
Come, without paying and without cost,
    drink wine and milk!
Why spend your money for what is not bread;
    your wages for what fails to satisfy?
Heed me, and you shall eat well,
    you shall delight in rich fare.
Come to me heedfully,
    listen, that you may have life.
I will renew with you the everlasting covenant,
    the benefits assured to David.

Praying with the Responsories

The Responsories provide the punchline, so to speak, to
the Readings. They enable us to carry away the essence of the
Readings. They are short and usually memorable. The following samples will show how much they can help our prayer life.
We might well look at the Responsories to the Readings

given above. The first is found in Evening Prayer of Tuesday in Week I:

Responsory for 1 John 1-3

Through all eternity, O Lord, your promise
    stands unshaken.
— Through all eternity, O Lord, your promise
    stands unshaken.
Your faithfulness will never fail;
— your promise stands unshaken.
Glory to the Father and to the Son and to the
    Holy Spirit.
— Through all eternity, O Lord, your promise
    stands unshaken.

Now we can look at the Responsory for the Reading from Tobit found in Morning Prayer of Wednesday in Week I:

Responsory for Tobit 4:15a, 16a, 18a, 19

Incline my heart according to your will, O God.
— Incline my heart according to your will, O God.
Speed my steps along your path,
— according to your will, O God.
Glory to the Father and to the Son and to the Holy Spirit.
— Incline my heart according to your will, O God.

The Responsory for the Reading from Paul's Letter to the Romans is found in Morning Prayer of Wednesday in Week II:

Responsory for Romans 8:35-39

I will bless the Lord all my life long.
— I will bless the Lord all my life long.
With a song of praise ever on my lips,
— all my life long.

Glory to the Father and to the Son
    and to the Holy Spirit.
— I will bless the Lord all my life long.

Finally, the Responsory for the Reading from Isaiah is
found in Morning Prayer of Tuesday in Week IV:

Responsory for Isaiah 55:1-3

Lord, listen to my cry;
    all my trust is in your promise.
— Lord, listen to my cry;
    all my trust is in your promise.
Dawn finds me watching, crying out for you.
— All my trust is in your promise.
Glory to the Father and to the Son
    and to the Holy Spirit.
— Lord, listen to my cry;
    all my trust is in your promise.

Praying with the Intercessions

The Intercessions offer a storehouse of relevant prayers at
our fingertips. They are new; they apply our faith to our life;
and they follow the rhythm of the Liturgical Year.

Are you looking for a Lenten prayer? You will find an
excellent one in Morning Prayer of Monday in the Second
Week of Lent:

Intercessions for Lent

God of power and mercy, give us the spirit
    of prayer and repentance,
— with burning love for you and for all mankind.
Help us to work with you in making all

things new in Christ,
— and in spreading justice and peace
throughout the world.
Teach us the meaning and value of creation,
— so that we may join its voice to ours
as we sing your praise.
Forgive us for failing to see Christ in the
poor, the distressed and the troublesome,
— and for our failure to reverence your Son
in their persons.

Do you want to give voice to your joy at Easter and your praise of God for his inestimable gift? Try the Intercessions for Morning Prayer of Friday of the Second Week of Easter:

Intercessions for Easter

All-holy Father, you accepted the holocaust of
your Son in raising him from the dead,
— accept the offering we make today, and lead us
to eternal life.
Look with favor on all we do today,
— that it may be for your glory and the
sanctification of the world.
May our work today not be in vain but for
the good of the whole world.
Open our eyes today to recognize our brothers
and sisters, and our hearts to love them,
— so that we may love and serve each other.

Do you wish to celebrate the triple coming of Jesus during Advent — his coming in history, in mystery (in our day), and in glory (at the Judgment)? The Intercessions for Evening Prayer I of the Second Sunday of Advent can be of great help:

Intercessions for Advent

Son of God, you will come again as the true
    messenger of the covenant,
— help the world to recognize and accept you.
Born in your Father's heart, you became man in
    the womb of the Virgin Mary,
— free us from the tyranny of change and decay.
In your life on earth you came to die as a man,
— save us from everlasting death.
When you come to judge, show us your loving mercy,
— and forgive us our weaknesses.
Lord Jesus, by your death you have given hope
    to those who have died,
— be merciful to those for whom we now pray.

Are you seeking a suitable prayer to honor Mary on
Saturday or on some feast? The Intercessions from the Memorial of the Blessed Virgin Mary will fill the bill.

Intercessions in Honor of Mary

Savior of the world, by your redeeming might you
    preserved your mother beforehand from all stain of sin,
— keep watch over us, lest we sin.
You are our redeemer, who made the immaculate
    Virgin Mary your purest home and the
    sanctuary of the Holy Spirit,
— make us temples of your Spirit for ever.
Eternal Word, you taught your mother
    to choose the better part,
— grant that in imitating her we may seek
    the food that brings life everlasting.

King of kings, you lifted up your mother,
    body and soul, into heaven,
— help us to fix our thoughts on things above.
Lord of heaven and earth, you crowned Mary and
    set her at your right hand as queen,
— make us worthy to share this glory.

AFTERWORD

A t the end of this little book on praying with the Church, it is appropriate to cite a few words of Pope John Paul II concerning the Church and prayer. They give a stamp of approval to the type of praying stressed herein and point up the value of praying with the Church. They were spoken on June 10, 1988, to a group of bishops from the United States.

> The universal Church of Christ, and therefore each particular Church, exists in order to pray. In prayer the human person expresses his or her nature; the community expresses its vocation; the Church reaches out to God. In prayer the Church attains fellowship with the Father, and with his Son, Jesus Christ. In prayer the Church expresses her Trinitarian life because she directs herself to the Father, undergoes the action of the Holy Spirit, and lives fully her relationship with Christ. . . .
>
> Everything human is profoundly affected by prayer. Human work is revolutionized by prayer, uplifted to its highest level. Prayer is the source of the full humanization of work. In prayer the value of work is understood, for we grasp the fact that we are truly collaborators of God in the transformation and elevation of the world. Prayer is the consecration of this collaboration. At the same time it is the means through which we face the problems of life and in which all pastoral endeavors are conceived and nurtured.

The call to prayer must precede the call to action, but the call to action must truly accompany the call to prayer. . . . In prayer we discover the needs of our brothers and sisters and make them our own, because in prayer we discover that their needs are the needs of Christ. All social consciousness is nurtured and evaluated in prayer. . . .

I wish to encourage you in all your efforts to teach people to pray. It is part of the apostolic Church to transmit the teaching of Jesus to each generation, to offer faithfully to each local Church [and its members] the response of Jesus to the request: "Teach us to pray" (Luke 11:1).

May all who use this book come to know where the best prayers are found and how to pray with the Church.

An Interesting Thought

The publication you have just finished reading is part of the apostolic efforts of the Society of St. Paul of the American Province. The Society of St. Paul is an international religious community located in 23 countries, whose particular call and ministry is to bring the message of Christ to all people through the communications media.

Following in the footsteps of their patron, St. Paul the Apostle, priests and brothers blend a life of prayer and technology as writers, editors, marketing directors, graphic designers, bookstore managers, pressmen, sound engineers, etc. in the various fields of the mass media, to announce the message of Jesus.

If you know a young man who might be interested in a religious vocation as a brother or priest and who shows talent and skill in the communications arts, ask him to consider our life and ministry. For more information at no cost or obligation write:

Vocation Office
2187 Victory Blvd.
Staten Island, NY 10314-6603
Telephone: (718) 698-3698